Foolproof Jumping Exercises

FOOLPROOF Jumping Exercises

For Horses, Ponies, Riders and Helpers

CAROL MAILER

J. A. ALLEN · LONDON

First published in 2013 by
J.A. Allen
Clerkenwell House
Clerkenwell Green
London ECIR OHT
www.allenbooks.co.uk

J.A. Allen is an imprint of Robert Hale Limited

ISBN 978-1-908809-04-9

A catalogue record for this book is available from the
British Library

Disclaimer of Liability
The author and publisher shall have neither liability nor
responsibility to any person or entity with respect to any
loss or damage caused or alleged to be caused directly or
indirectly by the information contained in this book.
While the book is as accurate as the author can make it,
there may be errors, omissions, and inaccuracies.

Edited by Jane Lake
Design and typesetting by Paul Saunders
Photographs by Matthew Roberts
Diagrams by Carole Vincer

Printed and bound in China
by 1010 Printing International Ltd

Acknowledgements

I am extremely grateful to all the riders who are shown in *Foolproof Jumping Exercises* and absolutely delighted they were so willing to allow the unflattering photos to be used as well as the good shots. This makes it so much simpler to recognise all the common failings, which is only possible, however, when they are illustrated so obviously on the page, captured by the camera of the wonderful Matthew Roberts; thank you Matthew.

Thanks too to the helpers who have volunteered to be guinea pigs for the duration of producing Foolproof and beyond. The enthusiasm, good humour, resignation and common-sense approach to their roles shines through in the photos, particularly as many of them are not 'horsey' by inclination. Long may they continue with their support.

I must also acknowledge my tendency to be repetitive with my advice throughout Foolproof, but I won't apologise because this is how I train. I'm a real nag, but I know it gets results.

It has also been very easy for me to work on the book with the patience and guidance of my editor, Jane Lake, and my publisher, Lesley Gowers, as I struggled to make my words of advice crystal clear.

I am also deeply thankful for my father who has been my helper with all my horses. With no formal equestrian training, his advice and common sense has been my foundation for any success I've achieved as a rider and trainer.

Long ago I received brilliant jumping training from the late Margaret Clarke and Margaret Millward who both showed me what was attainable, again as a rider and a trainer. Thanks to them I've done the work myself.

I know what you need and Foolproof will provide it.

Contents

PART 1

PART 2

PART 1

An introduction to foolproof jumping exercises for horses, ponies, riders and helpers

Introduction

The exercises in *Foolproof Jumping Exercises* have been well tried and tested and are designed to help improve jumping for all horses, ponies and riders regardless of their size, height, shape, age or experience, or any combination of these (Figures 1.1a–c). The book includes advice, suggestions and practical training tips that can help not only the riders but also the helpers

they choose to assist them. Significantly, if the guidelines in the book are followed faithfully, the helpers do not have to be experts themselves, but an eye for detail and a good helping of common sense are always useful.

The nature of the exercises will be an absolute blessing for beginners and their helpers to start with

Figures 1.1a–c Three very different horses, but they are each being asked to produce the same Foolproof quality canter to encourage the Foolproof quality jump. **a)** Becca insists that 17hh Christopher's canter stays workmanlike. **b)** Georgia and the 13.2hh Brooke are busy trying to produce a superior canter. **c)** Sarah works hard with the hefty 15hh cob Ben to keep him light and active too. The common denominator is hard work!

as the simplicity of the work required needs little explaining. The work may not be too easy to *achieve* at first, but it will be easy to *understand*. For the more advanced combinations, the exercises will help the improvement and consistency of good jumping practice.

As long as you don't try to change the techniques suggested when the jumps are raised, the confidence will keep improving and both you and your horse will soon start popping round courses far more effectively; you will find the jumping *easy*.

Most significantly, if things go badly at any stage you will know why or how you have got it wrong, and even more vitally, how to correct it without having an expert standing by scrutinising and analysing every hoof-fall.

Questions and answers

There are several commonly asked questions relating to this work.

Q Where does *Foolproof Jumping Exercises* fit in? How does the advice offered improve you and your horse? Should you use the work suggested purely on its own, or before or after the guidelines and detailed grids recommended in my previous book *Better Jumping*?

A *Foolproof Jumping Exercises* can stand completely alone as an infallible guide to encourage you to initiate or enhance all your jumping expertise whether you are a complete beginner or a 4-star event rider. The training recommended will be just as invaluable for complete beginners, for complementing any current training workouts, or for accentuating any skills already established. Whatever help you need to begin or improve your jumping you should find practical advice and solutions described clearly in *Foolproof Jumping Exercises*.

Q Should you always use a top trainer every time you try to jump?

A How nice that would be, but most riders have financial and geographical constraints, and would be unable to inhabit the ideal world of unlimited expert training and so the answer is: not necessarily. Two or three sessions with an expert would, however, set you up for understanding why you are doing the work suggested, especially if your helper is there to observe and continue the advice at home (Figures 1.2a–c).

Q Should you continue to use expert trainers or substitute a friend, partner, parent, i.e. a helper?

A It is best to use both if you can manage it. You need to know what is happening, and the trainer should be able to pinpoint a problem and solution

Figures 1.2a–c Your helper is there to keep an eye on you and give advice, which seems to be helping Kerry and Florence who are working very well through these jumps.

quickly and accurately but obviously it will be simpler to keep up the good work more frequently with a practical helper on the ground at home. If a helper is serious about helping you, this book's advice for helpers will soon give both of you the confidence to work successfully together.

From a safety aspect you should never try jumping without someone there. If they can lend a hand replacing poles or changing grids, they will soon become a vital ingredient for guaranteeing improvement, especially if they know what to say to give confidence rather than put a damper on things.

It doesn't always need a top trainer to tell you what's right or wrong or that it's time to just back off a bit, plain common sense from an informed helper will be a good alternative.

Q Should you use regular few-minute practices or have a major disruption to your routine to organise a professional lesson?

A Short sessions, little and as often as you can manage will be far more effective than trying to do too much in one go when it's likely that you and the horse will start to flag fairly quickly. A few poles and wings quickly set up will allow you to practise the canter easily and the three major exercises: the pat 'n' push, tripod, and tramlines (see pages 90–125).

If you are working hard enough, you won't be able to keep the power level up for too long. About half your session will be less effective as your energy levels drop, which is an expensive running out of puff if you are paying for a full lesson. Your common-sense view of the rate, or lack, of progress will tell you how your energy levels are holding up, and so will your helper, and it is perhaps a valuable lesson that to get the best out of the work, you should be as fit as you expect your horse to be.

It only takes a few minutes of quality exercise time to remind horse and rider to be neat, accurate, and active and to enjoy the work. It shouldn't be a penance, rather a privilege, to make it easy for your horse.

The quality canter

The basis for the success of these exercises is the quality canter and how to establish and maintain that canter will be explained on page 48. The same exercises, strategy, placements of poles and principles of the canter that will aid the novice combinations to get a good grounding in jumping will be just as effective for the more experienced and advanced combinations when tackling more demanding obstacles.

Once the canter is going well, you can start using the three more demanding Foolproof exercises which will ensure clean and accurate jumping whatever the situation (Figures 1.3a and b). These exercises will be very easy for your helper to set up and the only time you would need to adjust the distances to allow for different lengths of stride would be between the bounce grid and the pat 'n' push exercise. And the adjustments will be very minor, not a major reconstruction job like moving a long grid or changing related distances.

The Foolproof exercises

The work suggested in the following exercises is so straightforward you will be able to use the methods and positive attitude every time you work on your jumping and you will discover that gradually you will be meeting every fence on a better shot. They should be regarded as techniques for enhancing the skills, particularly the quality of the canter, rather than correcting particular problems. Their consistent use will tell you why or how you have got something wrong and, even more importantly, how to sort it out without having an expert standing by.

Each exercise has its own diagram showing the ideal and less than ideal route to take when riding the exercise.

If you are a newcomer to jumping, every exercise will be well within your scope to perform, because you can use poles on the ground instead of jumps and very small crosses: nothing scary at all. It is the route and canter that matter most. Don't feel that you have to

Figures 1.3a and b Anne and Guy, a little Highland chap, demonstrating a powerful take-off from a good canter.

try too hard to jump initially because then you might lose confidence in yourself. These poles and very low jumps will, however, ensure you develop and acquire all the steering and impulsion-producing skills required to turn yourself into a competent jumper when you actually start to leave the ground.

The principles to be established remain unchanged however big or small the jumps are and your helper will really need to be there from the word go as you will need every encouragement to keep trying when it appears that the work isn't working.

The only imponderable about the Foolproof exercises is the length of time it will take for them to be effective. It will be very easy for the more novice rider/horse to get dispirited if the repetitious nature of the exercises doesn't produce the right results quickly. It will be impossible to calculate when the exercises will be easier to perform and more effective, but it *will* happen. I named these exercises 'Foolproof' for just that reason; they are simply foolproof and will work but every combination will improve at a different rate.

Foolproof exercises are the ABCs of learning and producing better jumping, the sentences will happen all in good time.

Aims of the exercises

- However well you and your horse are going, don't get too satisfied. There are always fresh challenges to aim for and this set of foolproof exercises will help you exceed your expectations.

- Whatever standard you are, whether a serious experienced rider, a weekend competitor, or a complete beginner, utilising these exercises, albeit using different sized jumps or even just ground poles, will give you all the same practice, the same payback and the same opportunity to improve.

- The methods are totally uncomplicated and will encourage you to keep the horse working, look where you are going, and produce the quality canter required to jump well (Figures 1.4a–e).

- The series of very simple course exercises will develop your ability to allow your horse to meet every jump comfortably with a canter that has enough power for you to make a good job of it. Then the more concentrated work of the pat 'n' push, tripod and tramlines exercises will ensure that you use that quality canter to the best advantage.

Figures 1.4a–e A similarly top quality canter and jump from a horse and pony. Both riders have produced their mounts to execute the sort of elevated and high-powered canter which is so strong and active it looks as if they have actually grown an inch at the shoulder. **a–c)** Bex and 16.2hh Muddle, and (**d** and **e**) Coco and 14.2hh Spotty.

The benefits of the exercises

- These detailed exercises are ideal to help the supporter to encourage and the rider to practise the right sort of canter and jump under different circumstances. Turns, dog legs, related distances, spooky narrow fences, all the difficult elements can be discovered and dealt with as proficiently as the rider can manage, overseen by the helper on the ground.

- All the exercises suggested can be executed and practised by beginners using extremely small jumps, even poles on the ground. When you are confident with your canter and your steering you can raise the poles into crosses and then actual jumps.

- More experienced combinations will find that however well you are doing, these foolproof exercises will help you to jump higher, wider and more accurately (Figure 1.5).

- If you compete, at whatever standard, or just want to jump better at home, the work suggested is so simple and easy to set up you will be able to use the methods every time you practise jumping.

Figure 1.5 Becky and an extravagant Fin clear the water tray in great style.

- If your attitude to such straightforward work is receptive, gradually you will discover that you will be meeting every fence on a better shot and jumping it cleanly and with more power.

- These exercises improve your rhythm and impulsion so that your horse can get to his jumps with power and energy and not too far off the optimum take-off point.

- Every rider tells me that they have a job 'seeing the stride' and predictably my answer is 'Well don't look!' As soon as you start interfering to get the perfect take-off point i.e. *changing* your mode of riding, the horse will become confused.

- If you hook, i.e. try to shorten the stride by inappropriately sharp checking, or whoosh, i.e. try to lengthen and chase or rush the stride to organise the take-off point to the jump, he will lose impulsion. Both methods will ruin the consistency of the canter and interfere too much with the power stride pattern and you stand a good chance of making a hash of it, either hitting the poles, stopping, or running out.

  - There is a world of difference between steadying and pushing or hooking and whooshing. Experience and repeating the Foolproof exercises will help you to recognise just how much you can ask to receive the right response. If you can drill yourself to ride the same, whatever the situation, your horse should manage to jump very well without you being a control freak.

- The key to the success of the exercises is to produce the better quality canter to enable him to show you how good he is.

- Without fail, the work will help you meet your jumps on a better take-off point with more impulsion to make the job easy.

- You may be pretty good at jumping and win lots of competitions, but repeating the Foolproof work will help you win more.

- You may be a complete beginner to jumping, but once you are able to canter and steer, the benefits will be enormous.

- Don't forget, the exercises are all encompassing. They are suitable for each and every pony and horse, from a 12hh, or even smaller, pony to a 17hh plus horse.

- A benefit for your helper is that they will hardly have to move a thing. Even the most supportive friend, partner or parent will get a bit fed up if they have to put in too much physical effort! The jumps may go up or down, but actually shifting them and rearranging distances is kept to an absolute minimum.

The kit

- Although grids are used, they are very basic and don't involve lots of kit. If necessary you can make do with a few poles and half a dozen wings.

- If you haven't any kit available, hire an arena or school if you can, preferably at a venue that holds shows so that all the equipment you need will be on hand, and try to use the suggested course plan (see page 38) as a guide.

Self-analysis and self-help are the main goals of these exercises, but you must be honest with yourself and with whoever volunteers to be your long-suffering and much-maligned helper. Whatever stage you have reached, improving your ability dramatically every step of the way will be a certainty, as long as you stick to the Foolproof guidelines suggested. The work is simply that: foolproof. Try it!

The rider

However experienced a rider you are, you should always be watchful to ensure your ability and confidence don't become eroded and that your riding and presentation round a course stay as good as you can make them.

If you've been going well and have started to lapse a bit, this work will do the trick to help restore clear rounds, especially if you want to move your horse up a level.

Stay alert!

- You need to work hard enough to make sure he is not overfaced and be on **red alert** when you start something more demanding!

- Take nothing for granted, make it easy for the horse to perform well, be on **amber alert**, just in case.

- You must keep up the pressure on yourself and your horse to keep working hard and not have a casual **green light** attitude! (Figures 2.1a–i, see overleaf)

Tackling the exercises

- The exercises are not complicated and you will get out of them as much as you put in and know immediately if it's not going right. Your helper will be able to reinforce that opinion and offer a variety of solutions, one of which will work and get you both back on track.

- If you are an inexperienced novice rider or you have a novice horse, or if you are both starting out together, you will still find the work achievable. The simplicity of the effort required should be well within your scope as long as you are stable enough to trot or canter over a pole. Your steering, even in walk and trot as well as canter will be noticeably better.

- Whatever stage you have reached, *Foolproof Jumping Exercises* will help you move on, improving your ability every step of the way as long as you stick to the guidelines suggested

- It is the right attitude to the work which will guarantee success. The exercises are not so advanced that the novice riders can't manage them, and not so easy that the more experienced competitors won't find their riding ability improved by using them diligently.

- Foolproof exercises will pinpoint very clearly if the quality of the canter and presentation is good or not. And, most importantly, you and your helper will know too.

- They are primarily devised to help you *improve* the quality of the jumping canter and to utilise it to jump better.

- And then when you have that canter nailed and *feel* how it ought to be, the later exercises will show you how to best use it and improve your timing, balance and steering.

Preparation

- Study the advice in setting up suggested in the Be Prepared section on page 42. The guidelines recommended in the placing of the crosses and poles or jumps are important. They will help you to recognise how much pushing, gathering, holding the outside rein, using the steering rein, and all the subtleties needed to produce the power canter required, not just for half a dozen strides but all the way round the course.

- The work is so foolproof because the exercises are progressive and designed to encourage you to improve the consistency of the way you ride so that the presentation to every fence is as good as it can be.

Figure 2.1a–i Polly has practised this exercise many times which has possibly allowed Judith to relax slightly, and that is a big mistake. **a–g)** A bold jump in but Polly is landing a touch short. She changes her mind and says 'No!' Judith does well not to be shot off. Polly changes her mind again and decides to go after all giving a great push off the ground and Judith's recovery is terrific. **h)** Polly can be naughty, however, and is not best pleased to find Judith still on board and so deliberately kicks the cross out. **i)** Working well together and friends again; Polly proves she can be a nice cooperative girl!

- The exercises don't need to be too long to start with, you only need to keep the quality work going for half a dozen jumping efforts.

- If you run out of puff, you will let the horse's canter deteriorate if you aren't fit enough to keep working consistently. Why do you think the last fence topples after an otherwise immaculate round? Either you relax too soon or you're knackered!

- Check the diagrams for each work-out, once you start jumping some of the course as well as the end crosses or grid, four or five jumping efforts at a time is plenty to begin with. It will get easier and the exercises can be combined and get longer the more you practise; and you should be rattling fewer poles.

- If the horse is working harder and not going quicker, then logically it should be easier for him to jump bigger and wider rather than going faster and flatter. Faster and flatter usually means knock-downs, run-outs and refusals, all bad stuff.

- Work hard and the exercises are foolproof.

The rider's aims

Think about what your aims are. Maybe you want to jump a little higher? Perhaps you would like the spread extended a little more? Possibly you're keen to shave a couple of strides off a jump-off turn? Perhaps you want to improve your steering or you want a more consistent approach to the centre of the jump? (See Figures 2.2a–c)

The 'power canter' that the Foolproof work produces will help you give your horse every opportunity to meet his jumps far more consistently on a comfortable take-off point.

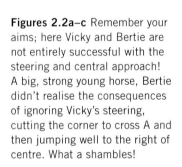

Figures 2.2a–c Remember your aims; here Vicky and Bertie are not entirely successful with the steering and central approach! A big, strong young horse, Bertie didn't realise the consequences of ignoring Vicky's steering, cutting the corner to cross A and then jumping well to the right of centre. What a shambles!

17

What's in a stride?

It is so easy to get carried away and become obsessive about the horse being within an inch of what you perceive to be the optimum take-off point.

Remember there is no such thing as a 'bad' stride. You might believe there is if the horse isn't on the button at each fence but, no, it's not so! These exercises will help you carry on producing the good canter which, in turn, will help you *recognise* that 'bad' strides don't really happen. If, however, you feel you aren't happy with the approach striding, you have three options.

If you try to organise this by checking or hooking, you will simply lose power and the stride you are looking for will have disappeared.

The three options

1. Your first option is to go for a 'longy', i.e. to chivvy the horse or pony to stand off the fence for a 'big' jump, by flapping and throwing yourself and your hands at the jump. The horse will immediately lose the power and impulsion when he needs it most. Option 1 = rattles and refusals. Unsuccessful! 1/10

   * **Correct response**: just keep riding the same quality canter. If your horse is able to stand off and wants to do so, he will have the confidence to throw in some extra effort because you haven't lost impulsion. Or he can choose to pop in a shorty to rebalance himself. Just keep riding in the *same consistent way* so he can decide what's best for the pair of you to clear the jump with confidence and power.

2. Your second option is when your horse is going to be too deep in to the jump to take off. As a consequence, you stop riding and stop producing the power necessary to help your horse be springy and neat. Option 2 = rattles and refusals. Unsuccessful! 2/10

   * **Correct response**: make the conscious effort to keep working hard and make sure you don't swing forward too early; get your timing right. The pat 'n' push exercise (see page 90) will sort out your timing so you allow the horse's head and neck to come up a bit more steeply towards your chest. If you bob down to him when you are deep to the jump, you will only add extra weight to his shoulders when he wants to be a bit snappier to make a clean jump.

3. Your third option is to be completely untroubled about where your horse or pony is going to take off and continue to ride a strong and active, but *not fast*, canter all the way to the fence. You can be indifferent to where the jump is in relation to your striding and keep riding the quality canter forward and up, ignoring where you originally hoped to arrive and making the best of not being totally happy. **Option 3 = good jump. Successful outcome!** 10/10 (Figures 2.3a–b, 2.4a–d and 2.5a–d)

Bottom row, opposite page and below **Figure 2.3a–d**
Horse strides: Phoebe can see that Wes is going to be a long way off the fence but she doesn't flap or go forward too soon, just keeps plenty of leg on, a good contact, and waits for him to come up into her chest. Wes gets 10/10 for effort.

Figure 2.4a–d Pony strides: Piglet gets in deep but Ellie keeps her leg on and her contact just as consistent as if the take-off point was perfect. She doesn't tip forward too early so Piglet has every chance to make a nice clean jump. Good result.

Figure 2.5a and b Pony strides: Bastion is on a longy, but Hannah doesn't change the way she is riding to encourage the big take-off. She keeps her consistent contact all the way to the fence and the resulting good jump is never in doubt.

The rider must ride so the horse can jump without being pulled about, hooked or placed to his fences. If you do the Foolproof work with confidence and consistency it will allow him to make any stride adjustments himself from a position of strength in the canter to get a good take-off shot to all his fences. All the work will help avoid misunderstandings between you and your horse while allowing him to get on with the job, and the economical and convenient vital ingredient to the success of the exercises would be wthe choice of helper.

Choice of helper

The Foolproof work needs to be done as often as you can manage it, and having a professional trainer standing by or visiting often will be very expensive and difficult to arrange. Hopefully if you are honest enough to admit to your mistakes and listen to the observations of a helper, you will manage very well, but only if you take off your rose-tinted spectacles and allow yourself to see you and your horse as you really are. So, what should you take into consideration when choosing a helper?

- Someone who is jumping successfully and knows a bit about what they are doing would be great, but not essential.

- Someone who may actually know little about horses or jumping, although not quite so ideal initially, will soon become the model helper if they

are available, sharp-eyed and can tell you truthfully what they see.

- A friend, partner, or parent will be absolutely fine if they are observant and honest, especially when you argue. And you will!

- Sometimes it may get a bit tricky when you fall out with your helper, particularly if you have a close relationship, and both parties should remember why they're doing it: it's a joint effort to help you jump more successfully.

- Your helper's assistance will be invaluable, and the observations offered will become more and more accurate as they get the hang of watching and reporting what they see. The comments suggested for the helper's use in the next chapter will soon get them on the right track. Of course there will be an odd situation which needs a more practised eye on the ground, but most of the time the observer will be able to communicate clearly enough what has happened so that you will be able to self-help and adjust.

- Don't forget that if you are doing more than discussed with your helper, it would be a good idea to shout out your intentions on the move (Figure 2.6a and b). Give them a chance to get out of the

Figure 2.6a and b Anne and Guy have completed an exercise and Guy feels good enough to carry on a bit further. Anne calls out her intentions to her helper and pushes on to the next jump. If you're going well, don't pull up, keep going and crack on!

way if necessary, they won't be very confident if they don't know where you're going next and feel at risk.

- Don't get picky with your helper! Unless they get in the way of the horse as he goes round, any helper is better than no helper, as long as they don't get drunk with power and start complicating things with their own theories. So, just the slightest note of caution: be careful to recognise if their advice contradicts that of an experienced and trustworthy trainer and starts to make things worse.

All the above points are why these exercises must be as uncomplicated and as foolproof as possible, and if they are used with the right attitude, they will be.

Foolproof Jumping Exercises will supply your helper with the information they need to assist you as the plain language will make it clear what they should expect to see and they will soon be confident enough to tell you when it simply isn't right.

It is an unenviable job, so just don't argue so much that they give up and abandon you.

When you get it right, it's all worthwhile (Figure 2.7).

Figure 2.7 Bertie and Vicky have got it right; a very pleasing outcome to the exercise they previously got wrong (see page 17). Even the sun has conspired to throw a shadow illustrating perfectly that they are in the middle of the cross.

The helper

If you have been chosen, or in fact volunteered, to be a helper to a rider, welcome to the world of jumping. Be assured help is at hand; *Foolproof Jumping Exercises* will not only guide the rider to analyse and improve the way they jump, it will teach *you* how to be competent and confident, to stand your ground and say the right things, even when the rider disagrees.

It is probable that your rider will always be a bit tricky and oversensitive to criticism if they are making a hash of things and will be more than ready to tell you that you know nothing. Let your rider know that you are aware of this because it is not much fun to stand in attendance, pick up and replace poles, and then be told how ignorant you are, but try not to fall out over it (Figure 3.1)! It is important that you are both prepared to recognise that you want the same thing: horse and rider to do better.

You can judge how well you are helping if the rider takes note and the horse starts to go better, and the foolproof nature of your help should be exactly that. It is not necessary to be an expert to say what you see, and there are some guidelines which will make sure that you don't say too many wrong things (Figure 3.2).

Helpers' guidelines

- Your judgment will be correct at least 85–90 per cent of the time; with the remaining 10 per cent or so, well, you'll just have to concede and gloss it over by saying that the rider went to the exercise without the helper being quite ready to watch.

- Remember how much your attendance will be saving them in convenience and hard cash so don't be too diffident.

- If you're not quite perfect, you will be a lot better than nothing, especially if the poles roll a lot to start with.

- And remember, you will soon start to learn too. Read the book and study the exercises for yourself.

- Go to one of your rider's lessons and listen to what the trainer advises. Most trainers are more than happy for their riders' friends to listen and learn.

- I *want* a child's parent or adult rider's helper to be involved at a training session to watch and

Figure 3.1 Expect an impatient, 'Hurry up! I'm waiting to come again,' even though it is they who have knocked the poles down!

Figure 3.2 Robert makes sure Becca knows how Christopher is taking off.

learn. They can then remind the rider to practise at home the things I've suggested, and I know if the exercises have been practised at home by how much they have improved at the next session.

- Even if you are a helper who doesn't ride, the exercises are described very clearly so it will help you to be aware of what you're looking for, and what you should say if it's not going well and the jumping is messy.

Observation and handy phrases

Most observations are purely common sense so don't be afraid to state the obvious, even if it's unpopular. Get as close to the action as you can and say what you see (Figures 3.3a and b). Try to remember the trainer's favourite phrases, they all have them, and parrot them ad nauseam, you will usually be right because the rider will keep lapsing and making the same mistakes.

At least one phrase, and usually several, will apply and be correct. Wade in from the beginning and set the tone, you're not meant to be just a dogsbody. Try to sound assertive and confident.

- Keep an eagle eye on the turns and the landings after every jump or grid.

- Watch the horse's inside hind leg; is it coming as far underneath his body on the corner as it does on the straight?

- Watch to see if the rider's shoulder drops or 'leads' on the turn.

(Figures 3.4a and b and, overleaf 3.5a–c.)

Figures 3.3a and b a) 'Emma, you've hit that pretty hard.' **b)** 'What on earth are you looking at; surely you should be looking where you're going next?'

Below **Figures 3.4a and b** Rosie's hind leg is working extremely well although Cath has allowed her inside shoulder to drop. Her outside rein is obviously very supportive.

Figures 3.5a–c a) '*Don't* go forward too soon to your jump.' **b)** '*Do* hover longer over your spread fences.' **c)** 'Cathy, stay level in the air. Fergus has jumped into the double beautifully, a nice non-jumping stride, then kicked the pole out behind. I bet it's his right hind that's the culprit. Dropped shoulder equals uneven weight equals dropped leg.'

Below **Figure 3.6** Helper Jill can spot exactly what's happening here. 'Nice jump from Brooke but Georgia, you're shooting your hands and your whole body is slanted too forward. Stay up more and keep hold!'

Things happen very quickly when your rider is in full flow, but even if you're not quite sure of yourself don't be afraid to keep up the warning commentary, it will remind your rider to keep doing the right things. It is very significant when you look at photos of head-on or rear shots that a droopy shoulder will usually result in the horse's corresponding leg not coming up quite as high as the other. It is easy for helpers to see what has gone wrong on paper, but when it occurs in real time, an untrained eye may not find it so easy to spot and you may be unsure if you have actually seen it, but there's no harm in adding 'Shoulder up' to your collection of handy phrases. (Figures 3.6 and 3.7a–d)

Figures 3.7a–d a–c) Georgia has made the same mistake again and this time she hasn't got away with it as Brooke nips out the side. Fortunately Georgia makes a good recovery from a pretty dodgy situation. **d)** Lesson well learned as Brooke shows how lovely she is when Georgia rides well.

Right **Figure 3.8** Pauline has her eye on Louie's back legs through the pat 'n' push bounce (see page 90). Even a non-horsy person would be able to see that his hind feet are nicely in line to push.

You will get better at seeing faults on the move, and your common sense will give you a fair idea of what has taken place, even if you can't initially spot it (Figure 3.8). Other phrases to add to the list are: 'Do look far enough ahead,' and 'Keep your weight in the stirrups level.'

Problems and responses

The major problems will always be when the rider wants to jump a fence and the horse doesn't oblige.

If the horse runs out, usually it will be caused by a badly angled approach or the rider has given with the hands and therefore the steering decision is left to the horse. If he is inclined to be naughty, cheeky or spooky, he runs out because he *can*. **Response**: try 'Keep hold'.

If the horse stops, the rider hasn't kept her legs on to keep encouraging the impulsion or she has given her reins away at the point of take-off. Or both! **Response**: try 'More leg, but no faster' and, again, 'Keep hold'.

Most of the time you will be correct, and the rider will probably recognise what is going wrong for herself, but it will give her a great boost to have her thoughts confirmed.

And if you're not always right in what you see, so what? You'll hardly cause a major crisis or setback as the incident has already happened and you will certainly be a huge asset. They are jolly lucky to have you in attendance to pick up poles and offer advice. You can't be *so* wide of the mark anyway.

'More leg, but no faster' will always get a better response no matter your lack of expertise so don't be apologetic if you feel a bit out of your depth. You're the one on the ground observing, learning and gaining the confidence to tell the rider what is happening, especially when they start to make a marked improvement, which of course, with your help, they will (Figure 3.9).

If the advice isn't working and the horse is going no better, just change tack and offer a different comment like, 'Keep hold' or 'You're too forward'; although the 'More leg, but no faster' observation usually sorts it. It is important that your rider recognises your judgment so that they will start to trust your eye without getting defensive about their ability.

Remember you're not there *just* to criticise but, when you do, it's nice to be tactful. On the other hand, don't be too sensitive or your role will be diminished.

My training criteria is based on my voice tone in a range from 1 to 10, when 1 is sweet and complimentary and 10 is, well, you don't want to go there! My number 8 voice has always been stringent enough to elicit the right response so far.

It will be a very successful session if rider, horse and helper finish in good humour with work well done, and it will be your attitude from the ground that will set the tone from beginning to end.

Figure 3.9 Cathy is explaining an error and is quite right and Vicky is more than happy to accept her judgment.

The Foolproof pony plan

Jumping exercises are usually concentrated on the horse and adult rider rather than the pony/child combination so it's about time there was more recognition of the huge difficulties experienced by the younger riders due to the variety of size of their ponies. And ponies are a law to themselves anyway.

Pony traits

Ponies can be nice and cooperative – genuine schoolmasters – but they can also be sly, lazy and headstrong. In general they behave as well or as badly as their larger relations and can buck, rear and nap, bite and kick in equal measure to horses but, on occasion, can be *more* wilful than horses.

The problems encountered when training difficult ponies are usually increased by the fact that they are often too strong for the children who ride them. Adults on ponies generally have great fun as they have chosen to ride a smaller animal but will physically be able to deal with any of the naughtiness that is peculiar to that pony. The small child rider on a pony the right size will often be unable to apply enough brakes or motivation until they have grown to the point of having to move on to a bigger animal. And then the cycle may start again.

Of course, most ponies recognise that they are well loved and will cooperate with their owners just as nicely as any well-behaved horse, but the opportunity will be there for them occasionally to pit their wits against their rider, just because they can. If they wish to be cheeky or disobedient, their rider may well not be strong or quick enough to outsmart them. Jumping fences will give them just such a chance to establish that they are in charge and only being ridden on their terms. Even when they love jumping, they may still play up from time to time: refusing, running out, napping to the gate or their pony friends. It's so very naughty and so disheartening for the child to be the duffer in the group.

The Foolproof plan will at the very least give them the knowledge and understanding to progress through the logical series of minimalist exercises and jumping over very small obstacles to establish that the pony should behave. Patience is the important ingredient and it's absolutely vital that the helper encourages the child with a wilful pony to be persistent rather than bullying, even if it seems to take forever. (Figures 4.1a–d, see overleaf)

At least Foolproof exercises start with such small jumps that a naughty pony can be led over them, and gradually you would expect them to start to improve if they realise they have no options. And even the early stages can be fun, especially if the child feels they are making a difference to the pony (Figure 4.2, see overleaf).

It should be fun!

It is essential that the basic Foolproof work for children is done repeatedly and practised until it becomes second nature. This may be tiring and tedious and I can understand why they get a bit fed up with the monotonous nature of the work; after all, how much fun is it to repeatedly pop over a pole on the ground or a small cross pole? They want to be doing more exciting things. But it's a good lesson in patience and they should be helped to understand that their reward will be the improvement in the pony; the sooner the basics are established and consolidated, the sooner they will be out and about having fun.

Once the rider has got the hang of producing the quality canter, the pony, whatever his size or length of stride, will be able to make any stride adjustments himself to get a good take-off shot to nearly all his fences. He and his rider will then be ready, and keen, to go out jumping and show off their progress. And you the helper, the parent, the 'wise one', must choose the rallies or outings carefully. You don't

Figures 4.1a–d a) The first time India and Flint tackle the spooky viaduct wall at number 14 on the course. In spite of India's efforts to keep Flint straight, he is already planning to lean in and be naughty. Her shoulders are level, her weight is to the outside and she does everything she can, but because he has already cut the turn to the jump after the cross at A, he has taken charge with a very cheeky result (**b**). This time (**c**) India has got to grips sooner with the strong and wilful Flint and has ridden a far better turn after cross A so that her presentation is heading straight to the middle of the jump, resulting in a lovely effort (**d**). And just note the push from those level hind legs.

Below **Figure 4.2** Little Ellie and Bertie are having fun: lovely pony, fabulous helpers, good contact, but Ellie should keep her head up.

want your child to have a disappointing time because the conditions are all wrong.

The long and the short of it

At some events, particularly in unaffiliated jumping, unless there is a competent course builder some of the pony tracks or courses may be very difficult for the majority of the class entrants unless they have worked seriously hard on their preparation schooling.

There must be a common-sense approach to tackling a course that has been set for any pony varying between say a dainty 12hh to a burly 14.2hh. The difference in the length of stride and scope between ponies measuring the same size may be enormous anyway, and will be even more exaggerated when the ponies differ in height as well.

It is not easy to devise a strategy for improving the jumping of children or adults riding ponies and very challenging to suggest more serious work for such different sizes and stride patterns.

Mostly the advice is given with a view to changing the distances in the grids or combinations of doubles and trebles.

Foolproof exercises concentrate on producing a better powerful canter and more accurate steering rather than getting obsessed with distances and take-off strides. The ponies and riders will have a better chance to improve their jumping without trying to stick to too rigid a stride pattern.

The trainer or helper must recognise that the riders, particularly the younger ones, need to be encouraged to be consistent in their efforts so that the ponies have a chance to sort out the approach and take-off points for themselves (Figure 4.3).

The rider might worry if the pony isn't in the place they perceive to be the perfect take-off spot at each fence; but as long as the helper insists that the work is practised, these exercises will help the rider carry on working every inch of the way to produce the good canter. As long as the rider continues to ride, even if they see that the approaching take-off stride is not going to be what they perceive to be perfect, the pony will still be able to jump well.

As a trainer, I feel that there is no such thing as a bad take-off stride. There is either a ridden stride to the take-off point or a *non*-ridden stride when the rider stops riding consistently or alters the way they are riding to try to 'help' the pony meet the jump where the rider wants them to.

Changing the way the pony is ridden just before the fence will inevitably result in the loss of impulsion. It won't work, and the pony rider has the

Figure 4.3 Kathy keeps a watchful eye on Ellie and Piglet and is ready to tell her to kick on to maintain the impulsion.

same three options to consider as their counterparts on horses if they are unhappy with the approach stride (see page 18). There must be a clear plan to keep riding consistently, i.e. the same, if they see that they are likely to be a bit far off the fence or a touch too close, and they need to make the right choice.

Remember, a pony being loose schooled nearly always gets to the jump on a 'good' stride. And if he doesn't, he will be able to shorten or lengthen to take the jump successfully. Repetition of all these Foolproof exercises will mean that if the rider works consistently to produce the quality canter it will help the pony to be able to adjust his take-off at the jump at the point most suitable for him to jump it easily. It doesn't have to be too difficult or complicated. The methodical approach will encourage all riders to achieve their potential when it comes to getting their ponies, or horses, up in the air safely and successfully and, similarly, ponies should be doing the same consistent work to achieve the vital better quality canter as the horses (Figures 4.3a–c).

The big advantage of the Foolproof exercises is that the ponies, just like the horses, are encouraged to work harder so that wherever their take-off point is in relation to the jump, they will be able to make a good job of it.

None of the exercises concentrate on the stride pattern through a double, treble or related distance. The main objective is for the pony to be capable and confident over the fence so he can land and have enough energy and power to keep going over whatever else is in front of him next, whether it's a made-to-measure perfect distance for that particular pony or a little more awkward.

As long as the rider has been drilled into always riding consistently, the pony will be able to shorten or lengthen to make the jump easier because the reliable work from the rider has given him the confidence and power to get up in the air.

If the younger riders and ponies develop the right sort of skills and don't get put off, they will make the transition to jumping, eventing, working hunter, team chasing and hunting far more successfully for having the jumping basics established at the earliest opportunity.

Figures 4.3a–c a) Missy is approaching the jump with a very nice active canter. **b)** Because she is going so well, Victoria anticipated Missy's take-off, looked down and went forward too early. Very precarious! **c)** A much wiser Victoria is looking well up and her timing is good as she waits for Missy's neck to come up to meet her chest; no bobbing this time.

Training children

The Foolproof pony plan won't work unless the trainer can establish the basic rules to help and encourage children to understand what they are trying to achieve. I won't train children unless the parent and/or helper is standing by me to listen, understand or query why I am asking their child to do certain exercises. They are the back up; they will be the ones to encourage the work to be practised between lessons. I will always know if they've practised at home before the next session. Or not!

I try very hard to actually *train* the younger riders by paying them the compliment of expecting them to want to improve.

I don't have much success with the children who look to their parents for sympathy when I try to encourage them out of their comfort zone. They obviously aren't quite ready to move on and would probably benefit from coming back when they are a little older. I can certainly understand their anxiety, it's such a high-risk sport and of course things sometimes go wrong.

The exercises suggested here are about as safe as I can make them, not only for children and ponies but for adults and horses too, and the work will be so straightforward that the young riders who lack confidence or who are riding a less than cooperative pony will soon find that it isn't so difficult after all.

Big frightening obstacles don't come in to it because a child must never be overfaced; it would be very counterproductive as you need them to trust you when you ask for that little bit more.

If, however, I do ask for a little more effort, I do expect them to give it a try, even if they don't succeed at first. If things don't quite go as I hope when we move on to a slightly more difficult exercise, and I stress the word *slightly*, it's very easy to retreat a stage and rebuild the rider and/or pony's confidence. As stated earlier, this work must not be a penance to all involved, it should be fun because if the youngsters don't think they're getting better, they will stop trying so hard.

I try not to differentiate between training methods for adults and children but of necessity I have to be a little more patient when explaining things to children, they are far more reluctant to give feedback if they aren't quite sure what I want them to do.

We won't get anywhere until they are crystal clear about our aims, and if it takes a bit longer for them to understand, it mustn't be a problem. There is no hurry to get the basic ideas established, and it's vital to do that, but I certainly don't want to be too restricted by the age of the child; if they aren't quite ready to take in what I am attempting to teach them, maybe waiting a while before starting the more serious training to improve their jumping would be a sensible option.

When they're interested in what they're doing, youngsters are like sponges, they absorb everything and I'm usually pleasantly surprised at how quickly they cotton on to what I want.

It is very gratifying to have them quote back to me something we worked on in a previous lesson as I know they've been thinking about what we've already achieved and are keen to show me that they've got it right and want to move on to the next stage.

The Foolproof exercises they've learned already with me should be easy to practise at home, especially with some help from the parent or friend, and they won't have to wait to arrange another lesson before they jump again. The more they can do at home at the right level, the better.

Being on a child's wavelength

Adults generally don't mind speaking up and querying why we're doing what we do, but often children are a little shy and don't want to appear less familiar with the usual equestrian jargon or terminology. It's no good trying to impress or baffle them with advanced 'horse talk' but everyday language works a treat – and of course it works well with adults too.

A *favourite* expression

'Shoo' is one of my favourite expressions, it says exactly what I want to get over and everyone understands immediately: move off, get going, keep working, more impulsion, work harder, get on with it, more leg.

A *favourite analogy*

My favourite analogy, one I use for all riders, however good they are, is Horse/Pony/Bicycle.

I ask riders to think about riding their ponies and horses as though they are riding a bicycle.

What happens if you stop pedaling? The bike goes forward but not so well! So keep pedaling, keep your legs working consistently (Figures 4.4a and b).

What happens if you don't steer? The bike goes where it likes, not where you want it to! Look where you want to go and keep holding on to the handlebars, the reins, so you can steer and take your planned route (Figure 4.5).

What happens if the bike gets too fast? You put the brakes on and slow it down! The same applies to your pony; take charge of the speed! (Figures 4.6a–d)

This is a very basic but good comparison and one that everyone can understand.

Of course I don't treat the younger children like babies, neither they nor their parents are going to learn anything valuable if I soft-pedal too much, but ordinary language is a very valuable tool.

Above **Figure 4.4a and b** Rebecca's legs keep 'pedaling' and insist that Poppy gets on with it.

Left **Figure 4.5** Turn your head like Georgia, look towards your next jump.

Opposite page **Figure 4.6a–d** Bertie the hooligan has tried to seize the opportunity to charge at the jump but Rosie is having none of it. She doesn't let him pull her over his shoulder, contains all his energy and gets a great take-off.

I do know the conventional phraseology, I learned to ride in the 1960s and it was altogether starchier and more 'correct'. I also remember being too scared to ask when I didn't understand things and I know that it stopped me progressing as quickly as the younger riders move on now.

If you pick up a British Horse Society Manual from that era, you will realise how far the horse world has progressed, not least in the language used. Certainly Pony Club handbooks contained a vast amount of common sense and practical knowledge, but unless you came from a horsy background they were unfathomable as some of the terminology came straight out of the 1930s; you needed a dictionary!

Perhaps a lot of the phrases I use have gone a touch too far the other way, but I know the children understand what I mean when I ask them to do things, and I don't have to rely on a fifty-year-old vocabulary to tell them how.

I've even been coerced into 'high fives' by some of my younger riders when they've done a particularly difficult exercise successfully. Communication is everything, and it's wonderful to share their delight in a job well done, even if it leaves me faintly self-conscious!

The Foolproof exercises are absolutely ideal for every combination and size of ponies and their riders. They will clarify the skills required without complicating the methods needed to do well and are identical to those the horses are doing. Ponies will achieve the same benefits as the horses as long as they try just as hard with the same thoroughness and attitude to the work.

Keeping up the standards

Once the horse and rider are going well, how will they manage to keep up the standards? Quite simply it's a case of not getting over-confident and making sure things get put right when they go wrong.

Over-confidence

Riders who become too satisfied with their performance are very rapidly going to get their comeuppance. They will find their performance soon starts to deteriorate due to a tendency to complacency. Certainly a combination of horse and rider that keeps winning classes can be forgiven for being slightly relaxed about their ability, *but* the day will come when they make a silly mistake, forget what they're doing and stop riding quite as effectively.

Even top riders at the Olympics or World Cup Show Jumping finals have been known to forget the course or start before the bell. These riders have stables full of top horses, ride and school several horses a day, compete at all the top shows and have so much ring practice that there should be no chance of getting the basics wrong. And yet they do because it's human nature to relax when things are going well; everybody does it. It is when riders relax a little too much, however, that it then becomes a no-win situation in more ways than one. They descend from being on top form and jumping lots of clear rounds, to finding odd errors starting to creep in.

Professional riders will soon sort out any hiccups very quickly, it's their living and they don't make many mistakes, it's too expensive.

But what about the weekend competitor – riding at local jumping level – who discovers that the good results they've been achieving start to diminish? I am not talking about habitual or specific problems like sudden or nasty refusals or run-outs but more particularly things like a pole down here, a run-out there, or a sloppy or missed turn. Their performances are just not quite good enough, just not quite up to scratch, just not *consistent* enough to keep jumping as many clear rounds as they have been.

If you have been doing well enough previously then ask yourself these questions.

- If your ability is not restricted by nerves or anxiety in a show or schooling situation, then how can you recapture your form?

- If your horse has no hang-ups about spooky fillers or water jumps and his normal stride pattern is conventional, and if there is no struggle to make the distances easy in combinations or related distances, why is he making the odd mistakes?

- What is going to help restore his accuracy?

With no really obvious or major errors to address, any kind of special remedial gridwork will probably be unnecessary, and yet something needs to be done before things get worse and the horse starts to develop a real problem. That 'something' is that riders should constantly be reminding themselves how they *should* be working, and the Foolproof exercises will do just that.

Stopping problems in their tracks

When you realise that you are going slightly off form with your jumping and clear rounds are hard to come by, the obvious solution is to get help from someone more knowledgeable: your experienced and trusted trainer.

Ask your trainer what you can be practising at home before you have another lesson. A sensible trainer will advise some simple but effective work to keep reminding you how effectively you could still be working when your everyday helper is not an expert.

Foolproof exercises together with your helper will encourage you to stay on track between lessons when you can't manage to work with your expert as often as you would like. Even something as basic as set-distance canter poles are so easy for anyone to arrange and work over, and used with the right attitude will keep both you and the horse from sliding back before your next training work-out.

There is much more you can do to help yourselves and it doesn't have to be complicated, just a few crosses or small jumps strategically dotted about, but immensely helpful when used with the correct approach.

These exercises or self-help sessions need to be plain and clear, foolproof in every way. It would be pointless for you to be struggling to improve things unless the homework prescribed is obvious and achievable.

The exercises suggested are so straightforward that you will be able to use the poles and grids to analyse why you are making mistakes and, far more importantly, learn how to correct them quickly and easily.

The helper's role in maintaining standards

Remember helpers, you aren't just on duty to shift or pick up poles (Figures 5.1a and b). You will play a vital role in ensuring your rider does not start to get over-confident and will be able to see when niggling errors creep in, probably some time before the rider does (Figures 5.2a–j, see overleaf). Once the practice fences are in place, there should not be too many knock-downs to deal with, your main duty will be to observe and report. So have the confidence to tell your rider what you see when the exercises are being performed so they will be able to use that feedback to adjust and improve how the horse is going in order to keep up their standards.

Remember your repertoire of stock phrases and suggestions, and keep up the running commentary with the ones you feel fit the bill.

Figures 5.1a and b Anne's role isn't just a pole placer; she's there to offer help and advice too.

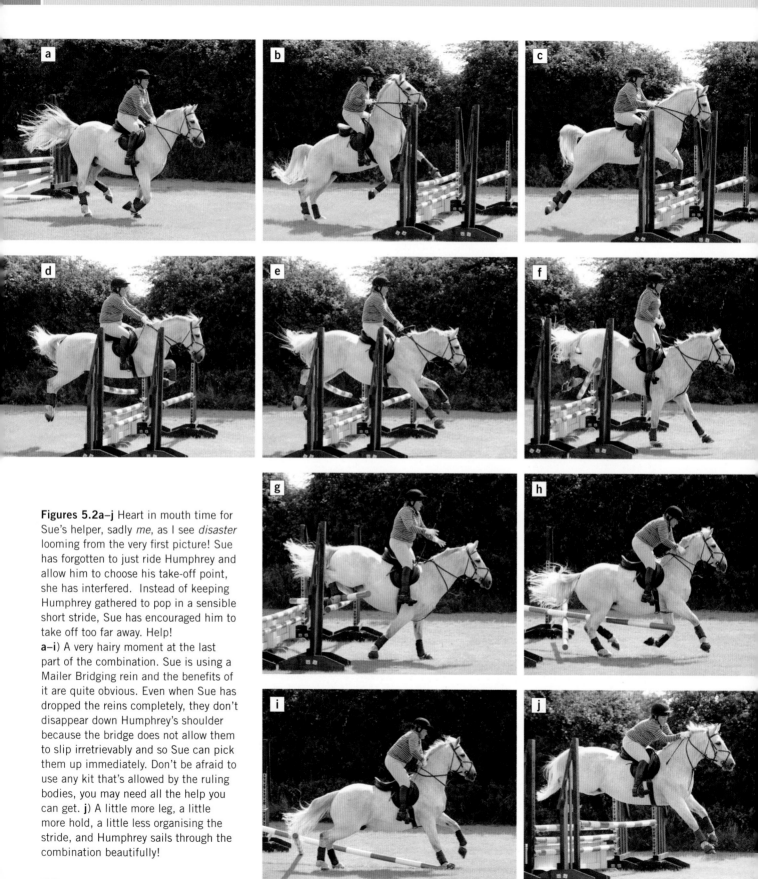

Figures 5.2a–j Heart in mouth time for Sue's helper, sadly *me*, as I see *disaster* looming from the very first picture! Sue has forgotten to just ride Humphrey and allow him to choose his take-off point, she has interfered. Instead of keeping Humphrey gathered to pop in a sensible short stride, Sue has encouraged him to take off too far away. Help!
a–i) A very hairy moment at the last part of the combination. Sue is using a Mailer Bridging rein and the benefits of it are quite obvious. Even when Sue has dropped the reins completely, they don't disappear down Humphrey's shoulder because the bridge does not allow them to slip irretrievably and so Sue can pick them up immediately. Don't be afraid to use any kit that's allowed by the ruling bodies, you may need all the help you can get. **j**) A little more leg, a little more hold, a little less organising the stride, and Humphrey sails through the combination beautifully!

Figure 5.3 When Sue presses the right buttons Humphrey can choose his own strong take-off point and is spectacular in his jump.

PART 2
THE FOOLPROOF EXERCISES

The Foolproof course plan

Check the Foolproof Basic Course diagram on the page opposite.

Please note that in this and all the exercise diagrams the letters A and B are labelling the cross poles, the jumps, on the short side of the school, *not* the position of those crosses, i.e. they are *not* representative of dressage markers.

The plan is particularly designed to be a schooling course constructed to include nearly all the difficult routes and problems a course builder might throw at you. Remember that this is meant to help you recognise any of your particularly weak areas that you may need to concentrate on improving.

- Perhaps you find it difficult to ride a straight line when you're not guided by the boundary fence or you allow your horse to wiggle or cut in on the corners.

- Perhaps you don't look far enough ahead so that your steering is erratic.

- Perhaps you allow the horse to go too fast and don't have the confidence in yourself to steady him.

- Perhaps you need to use more leg to keep him moving forward instead of allowing his energy to fade.

I do listen to my riders so I know what you don't like, and I never make light of your worries. So often I hear you say 'I hate planks' or 'He always spooks at a water tray' or 'I can't do "skinnies" or triple bars'. Sometimes you feel that a particular colour filler will be your undoing and go to pieces if that colour is featured at a show.

My job as a trainer is to encourage you to overcome your reservations and treat every obstacle as being as achievable as an easy cross pole, even if it's a jump you have doubts about.

I'm very fortunate to be able to build the courses that I feel will give you most practice and to contain the bogey fences that so many of you dislike or find difficult. Included in this course are several sets of bright planks, spooky fillers, a water tray, 'skinnies' i.e. narrow jumps, doubles on both reins, dog-leg approaches, related distances and demanding turns. In fact, there are so many opportunities to take a dislike to what is in front of you!

If you have a problem during a round at a show and are eliminated, you won't usually have the chance to solve it. Even when the judges are kind and let you have another go or two before leaving the ring, you'll probably be gonged out before you've sorted out the setback calmly.

It is not just difficult or inexperienced horses who need understanding and improving, sometimes you, the rider, can be the cause of a problem too, especially when your confidence has taken a hit. But if you practise in private you can find the solution and keep repeating it until you are confident the problem has been consigned to the past.

When someone comes for a first training session, I like to find out tactfully what they've been doing and

Foolproof Basic Course diagram

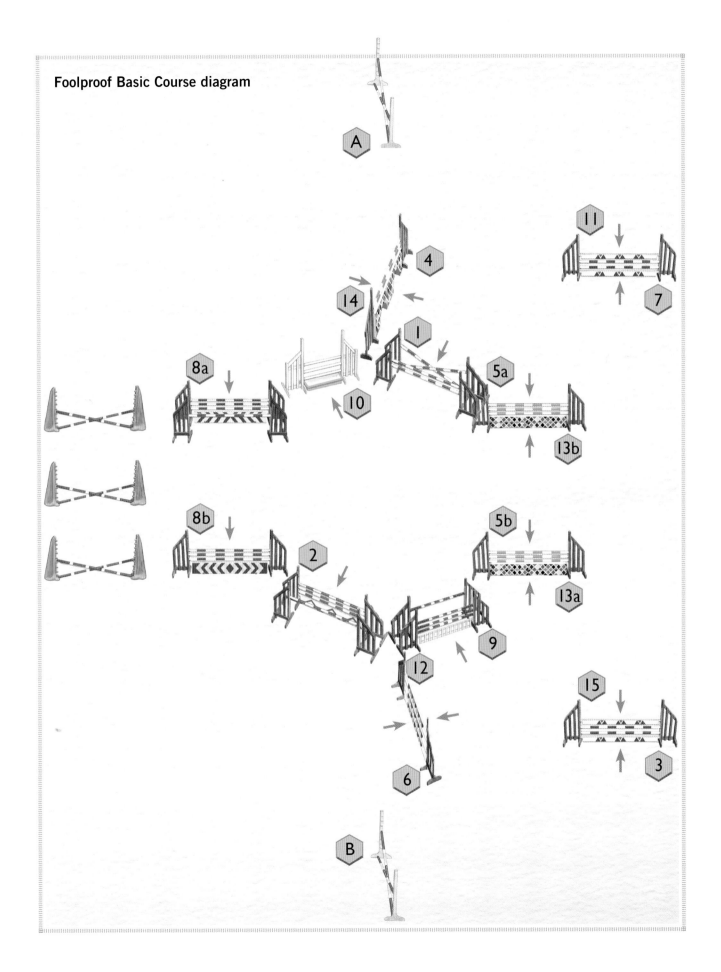

what size jumps they want to tackle; not for any other reason than because it's helpful to have the jumps already set at the right size.

Nearly every rider is apologetic as they seem to think they should be jumping bigger fences and they say something like 'We're only doing 75 or 85 or 95cm', 'He's only seen a small fence', 'He's never seen colours before', etc. They are just making excuses for not going well before they start. I therefore always begin by building slightly lower than their stated comfort zone size.

The confident or more professional riders who say they are jumping 1.1m or 1.2m plus are treated just the same and I always start slightly cautiously before increasing to the size that they think they are good at.

When you are a helper, keep that in mind. It is much better to put the jumps up when your rider is going well than put them down because they have started too ambitiously and are going badly.

All I want you to do is improve and ride and jump better, whatever the starting point; we should all have the same aim. Once we have the measure of each other and work in harmony the Foolproof course plan will if taken step by step, however it's adapted, help every rider do just that.

Adapt and improvise

If you haven't enough kit to build a course, take note that the course diagrams and exercises advise you to practise only a few jumps at a time not go straight round the whole thing. So do use jumps where you can for each exercise, and try to have enough poles strategically placed in the position of the jumps on the course plan. If you just don't have enough kit even for this adaptation, be prepared to get off and assist your helper to change things round after you're happy with each suggested sequence. Don't expect them to do all the hard work while you just sit on your horse. And remember, if you don't have the equipment to build jumps, you can use just ground poles to represent them.

All the jumps have been carefully placed to help you achieve the maximum benefit from the exercises, and will definitely allow you to see and feel immediately where and how you may be going wrong.

Remember, that the plan is ideal, *not* compulsory. I build it because I can, and it is perfect for all my riders, but you can only do what you can do, so compromise sensibly. And, as mentioned before, if you don't have any kit at all, hire a course or try to borrow friends' jumps. Don't feel you have to reproduce the course prescribed in its entirety to be able to practise. The Foolproof exercises can be adapted to any course, even if it's different to the plan suggested here.

There will always be turns or corners to negotiate, no course will be entirely in a straight line, so check out the diagrams to see where the crosses are in relation to the turns. Then try to use crosses or ground poles where they will have most effect when used with the other jumps, however they are set; if they guide or encourage right angles or three-quarter turns to the actual jumps the exercises will still be very valuable.

A simple cross at each end of the school or practice area, plus a short bounce grid of three crosses on the long side will remind the rider how they should be working and will help give them a 'feel' for the canter needed to help produce reliable and dependable clear rounds.

Crosses are best because you have to be accurate with the steering to jump them in the middle, and if you are slightly off centre or too casual in your approach you will knock them down, and you will know why: slovenly presentation, poor steering or no impulsion, and possibly all three at the same time.

If you haven't enough material, forget the bounce grid but *do* go for the crosses at each end so you can negotiate them before and after a turn.

The crosses really are a foolproof aid even if you are on your own or your helper is not a practiced trainer. But if you are working alone, adapt. If you keep kicking the crosses out, decide why.

- Are you off-centre and jumping at the highest point?

- Are you too fast and forward?

- Are you cutting the approach corner and still slanting when you take off?

Remember what you're doing badly, make your mind up to sort it out, and then substitute ground poles instead of crosses, you won't then have to keep getting on and off if you clip them.

You will certainly be working for a while before you get to the point when the horse meets everything spot on, so don't be too hard on yourself in the meantime. Just a single pole will show you if you are producing the right sort of power canter or not. If when you arrive at the pole in canter the pole lies in the centre of the horse's stride, *without* you trying to engineer it, you will have achieved the power canter, and the horse will have made his own adjustment to meet it comfortably.

If you have to use poles on the ground in place of the jump positions they will be more than adequate to show you if you are meeting the obstacles on a strong, active and accurate stride. The poles will be very representative of the jumps and you will know how well you are doing if you meet them so that they are in the middle of your horse's stride. And if you don't know if that is happening, your helper will certainly be able to tell you if you're doing well enough or not.

If your kit or space is limited, pick out the particular aspects of the course you feel you need to practise and try to reproduce those areas one at a time to practise over. Get one sticky situation improved and then assist your helper to move the jumps or poles so that you can practise the next moves where you think you will find yourself out of your depth; don't let your helper get the impression that she is just a skivvy.

The diagrams of a full jumping course in the following exercises will show how to add and incorporate a bounce grid of three simple crosses down one long side, plus a small cross at each end of the practice area to encourage you to use every opportunity to do exactly the sort of work you should be practising to get the better canter.

As you progress, it will be very easy to adapt the grid and end crosses to set up the pat 'n' push, tripod and tramline exercises suggested later.

Even if you don't plan to go out and compete it doesn't matter, this course will still enhance your skills as a rider and you and your horse can have so much fun improving. So many of the riders I train get immense satisfaction from jumping better, whether they go to shows or not. A desire to compete should not be the only reason for wanting to progress.

Tried and tested

I have checked and tested every single exercise myself to make sure they work well before I ask my riders to do them. You never stop learning and hopefully never stop improving; and you need to be on the ball to keep up with the course builders.

Show jumping has evolved over the last two or three decades. There are more arenas and show centres and more opportunity for riders to get out and do more. The courses are far more technical and demanding, especially as so much jumping is held on an artificial surface in an enclosed arena. Every inch of space is utilised and there is little room for error. You need a relentless consistency to do well, and the Foolproof exercises are designed specifically to encourage this.

The benefit of using the course plan is that you can do the work in stages, and there's no need to move on until the particular skills of a particular exercise are well established. Eventually you will be able to string all the work together to complete a whole course, but the gradual process will immediately let you know if it is going wrong, and how to get back on track again.

The turns vary in degree of difficulty, and obviously the horse will start with the easier options first, but there is scope on the course to practise just about everything you would need to do, especially when combined with the Foolproof additions using the Polyjump grid fences.

Because the Polyjumps are plastic I feel I can be a bit bolder with what I ask from the riders. If mistakes are made, they are not usually painful mistakes. I'm so fanatical about these jumps that Polyjumps have actually named them the Carol Mailer set as I never work or start a training session without them.

A challenge for every individual

The whole course is designed to be tackled by all shapes and sizes of horses and ponies and be equally challenging for each and every one. If the quality of the canter and the consistency of the riding is good, all should do equally well over this long and demanding course. The jumps should be a comfortable size for the rider. The whole point of the Foolproof exercises is to improve your riding, not put you under strain. Getting stressed and overfaced is pointless. You and your helper will know when you want, and are able, to jump bigger fences.

Obviously more experienced combinations will want to jump bigger fences, and why not? But if they combine the size of their jumps with the right attitude to the Foolproof work suggested, they will discover just how much scope they actually have. And they will be able to do so much to improve their jumping with a bit of common sense and an honest and forthright helper.

Be prepared

Equipment

What extra equipment do you need to keep up the jumping training at home? If you have access to an arena you will be able to adapt all the Foolproof exercises suggested to fit in to the space you have, even if the arena is smaller than that shown in this book. You might have to cut down on the number of jumps to fit them in, but you will still be able to have diagonal and straight lines and corners and turns, even with fewer fences.

If you are working in a field, try to mark out an area to work in to keep your approaches on the short side; if you make long swooping turns the benefit of the work is lost. Big areas and long run-ups give you more time to get it wrong, not more time to get it right.

- A schooling area of around 60–70m by 30–35m would be ideal and poles at right angles in each corner would be fine (Figure 6.1).

Figure 6.1 Mark out your ideal schooling boundaries with old poles.

- If you have a fence or hedge to work against, do use it. It will be a tremendous asset to have even one fixed boundary when you are negotiating all the exercises suggested.

- If you hire a course, however it's built, you should still be able to adapt the suggested Foolproof exercises to produce the same high-quality canter that will give you the better jumping expertise.

- The addition of only a few crosses and poles to *any* course, strategically placed, will give you everything you need to analyse your riding, discover where your shortcomings lie and, most importantly, what to do about it. Foolproof will give you the confidence to self-help and correct your faults as well as schooling and improving your horse's way of jumping.
  - The jumps in the arena are placed particularly to illustrate what you should be trying to achieve by the sensible use of the blue crosses at each end, on the short sides, and the red crosses down one long side.

Distances

Use a tape to measure the bounces, don't rely on pacing, and set the distances as follows:

- horses over 14.2hh – 12ft (3.7m)

- 14.2hh – 11ft (3.4m)

- 13.2hh – 10ft (3m)

- under 12.2hh – 9ft (2.7m).

One-stride related distances or doubles should be twice the bounce distances to be fair on the various size ponies.

British Showjumping courses

British Showjumping course builders have an excellent record of suggesting the correct related distances for doubles or combination obstacles to suit the ponies' ability, but ponies are a law to themselves and are well able to shuffle in extra strides or stand off alarmingly well in their efforts to get over the jumps.

The BS course builder notes on course designing are very clear on the distances advised for different-sized ponies, but unless they are specified-height classes, distances will be the same for ponies of 14.2hh and all sizes under that height. They must negotiate the stride pattern and distance as best they can.

The distances set for horse classes too will be the same for any size horse over 14.2hh.

Trailblazer courses

Trailblazer shows too are going to build the same track for all sizes for 14.2hh and under; the only stipulation for the courses will be the maximum height built in each class with no mention of the related distances, which will be set at the course builder's discretion. So any related distances will have to be negotiated by any size pony up to 14.2hh.

Equally challenging will be the horse distance set for any size over 14.2hh.

Unaffiliated jumping

Many show centres, village shows, riding schools, livery yards and hunt or charity events will run their own unaffiliated show-jumping classes, both for horses and ponies. You would hope that they would sensibly use the BS or Trailblazer rulebooks to guide their officials to have a common-sense approach to keeping the standards up, but it would only add to the costs to employ a qualified course builder. If they muddle on and build less-than-perfect courses and you want to have fun and compete, Foolproof will help your horses and ponies cope with the less-than-perfect related distances.

Whatever type of show you want to jump at, the smaller ponies and horses must just do their best when the distances don't suit them, either stretching uncomfortably or putting an extra stride in.

Don't forget either that the extra-long striding horse and pony will also find the distances difficult and will need to shorten their strides accordingly.

Foolproof exercises recognise that you and your horse or pony will be expected to jump around courses that are not going to be tailor made to suit the different stride patterns. It will be the impulsion and energy produced which will make the jumping effortless, not the striving to reach an impossible or unsuitable distance on one long, fast, hair-raising stride, or the putting on of the brakes fiercely to shorten the stride so you don't get too close to the next element.

All the work prescribed will make the canter active and the horses careful, and most importantly will prepare them to still jump well when the related distances at shows are far from ideal.

The Foolproof conventional one-stride distances are set on either the horse (24–25ft [7.3–7.6m]) or 14.2hh pony (22–24ft [6.7–7.3m]) measurements because that is what you will probably find when you compete. (Figures 6.2a–c, 6.3a–c and 6.4a–c)

The Foolproof exercises for the quality and reliability of the jumping canter have ensured the horse and ponies in Figures 6.2–6.4 make a good job of the jumps even when they have different stride patterns. They have all been ridden well and allowed to sort out their own take-off point from a position of strength and consistency.

The red crosses on the long side and the blue crosses at each end are the important components of the exercise, and it will pinpoint very clearly if the canter is good enough or not. Most importantly, the exercise will ensure you and your helper know if you're going well enough or not. If it's right, you will jump better. If it's not good enough, the jumping won't improve and will probably deteriorate. The dependable helper will soon become indispensable and, armed with *Foolproof Jumping Exercises*, will be able to learn quickly how to say the right things at the right time.

Figure 6.4a–c Fin at 16.3hh finds the 25ft (7.6m) distance just a touch short for his one stride and Becky needs to tactfully hold him off the second jump.

Smart jumps

All the smart, or show standard, jumps are there to prove that if you are working really hard on the corners to get a good canter you will get a good shot to all the jumps, even the ones you instinctively dislike.

- You will have fewer knock-downs or rattles, a more comfortable take-off point, and a lot more power to keep going round your courses.

- You won't need to wonder if you are doing the right things, the improvement in your horse's ability will be all the proof you need to convince you that you are on the right track.

- If you have already discovered the benefits of steady progress by working with the conventional gridwork and a professional trainer, the Foolproof work-outs will assist you to further improve the consistency of your jumping by helping yourself more. And if you are a beginner, then it's the 'way to go'!

- If you hire somewhere with a course to work on, the blue crosses on the short sides are the ones to try to replicate. It will be fine to use a pole on the ground in place of a cross if you have to.

- There probably won't be room for the bounce crosses at the side because most arenas are rectangular rather than square and the courses built for hire won't allow for the schooling options I prefer. The courses will be set to take up the whole width of the arena.

- It should normally be acceptable to use the crosses on the short ends as it is very unusual to set course jumps squarely across the ends.

- If you can't copy the suggested course, don't worry, do the best you can and don't let the different course put you off.

- If the crosses at the ends of the school are ridden well, the jumps off the corners, wherever they are situated, should be met with power, energy, and

Opposite page
Top row **Figure 6.2a–c** Brooke and Georgia put two neat, active and similar strides in on the 23ft (7m) distance and have plenty of room for a good jump over the next element.

Lower row **Figure 6.3a–c** Hannah and Willow, a bit bigger than Brooke, take on the 23ft (7m) distance in one stride, and although a little far off the last jump the push from the hind leg is very well produced and they soar over.

from a consistently comfortable take-off point (Figures 6.5a–d and 6.6a–c). Just remember why you are riding over the crosses or ground poles: they are there to help you; don't consider them a nuisance that is in the way of you getting on round the turn.

- The exercises are not complicated and you will get out of them as much as you put in.

- It's an attitude to the work which will guarantee success. They are not so advanced that the novice riders can't manage them, and not so easy that the more experienced competitor won't find their riding ability enhanced by using them diligently.

- The more advanced riders will probably want to tackle bigger jumps and, similarly, it won't matter how tiny the novice rider's jumps are set. The basic requirements of the work, the aims and use of the exercises will remain the same whatever size you are jumping.

Figure 6.5a–d Andrea knows this is not good: poor sprawly canter, not enough leg; Andrea is giving her rein so there is poor contact and no power for Holly to sort out her take-off point. It is a bit of a mess and not very comfortable.

Figure 6.6a–c The handy phrase here would be, 'More leg, but no faster', which will result in a better canter, better leg, better contact, better jump. Notice how much further Holly's hind leg is underneath her in this second sequence. Andrea and her helper have conferred, recognised what was wrong and sorted it out.

The horse's dress code

Your horse's dress code should be exactly the same as you would use at a competition. Don't neglect anything because you are only practising. If you respect the exercises, you will be jumping clear rounds more and more often, so keep him safe and protected.

- Boots or bandages (if you use them).

- A running martingale, or breastplate, is a must.

- My Mailer Bridging Reins.

- A bit that allows you to keep hold without being towed.

- Studs are advisable when jumping on grass, even if they are a nuisance to put in.

- A stud girth is also advisable because you're going to get your horse's front legs tucked a bit higher and more folded and you don't want his underside bruised, even without studs in.

Don't leave anything to chance, there's no need. You want to be ready for anything.

EXERCISE 1

The foundation exercise

The quality of the canter

You must learn to produce and develop the right sort of good-quality, high-powered canter, neither the faster dressage canter nor the slowed down cross-country gait; the better jumping canter has an identity of its own.

This Foolproof foundation exercise is so basic that it could easily be discounted but if it *is* disregarded you will fail to make good progress. It is hard work to get it right and to keep it up but the harder you work, the easier your horse will find the jumping. **It is *so* important to get right that before detailing the exercise itself the quality canter must be defined**.

The first step is to actually understand what the experts mean when they stress that the 'quality of the canter' is paramount. So much has been discussed, written, analysed, paraphrased and advised about the quality of the canter that many riders are parroting the phrase and hoping they will achieve it by wishing rather than working harder.

A sensible definition of the quality jumping canter is a canter from which your horse should be able to jump well, each and every stride he takes if necessary, and a better quality canter will give him more impulsion and help him meet the jumps on a good take-off point, both of which will ensure the jumping improves massively.

Non-professional riders, however, are generally not quite sure what they are looking for and how to achieve it. You need to understand how to recognise it, how to get it, and how to maintain it consistently, at least for the period of time to complete a course of jumps. You need to get the right 'feel' for the canter so that it's an automatic process to set off in the right mode.

There are foolproof methods for achieving and recognising this canter fairly easily, but the tricky bit is maintaining that canter and producing it all the way round a course. Although you have to steer as well, there should be no need to relax the relentless canter just because you need to look where you are going next.

The jump will interfere with the actual canter and you need to be pretty quick to re-establish the right power and energy as soon as you land, certainly before the next jumping effort. If the quality of the canter deteriorates the further the horse goes, then the quality of the jump will diminish too.

How to produce and maintain the quality canter

- Most importantly the horse must always be ridden from the leg into a supporting contact and encouraged to canter round the corners with a powerful hind-leg action.

- The canter should be strong and active, not fast.

- If the hind leg starts to mince, shorten or stutter on the corners, i.e. going up and down more or less on the spot instead of coming forward as effectively as it does when working on the straight, the quality of the canter will just not be good enough.

- The helper must watch the horse's hind leg like a hawk to see if it is coming as far underneath his tummy as it does when he is going straight (Figures 7.1a and b).

Figures 7.1a and b Karen and Miller could jump anything from this sort of power canter; Miller's hind leg is well under his body.

- The corners must be ridden confidently and robustly, *not* politely and tactfully, you should be looking for more energy produced around the actual corner and then trying to maintain that power as you straighten up.

- Whichever hind leg is further underneath you, even if it's not the one you prefer and he is going disunited, disregard that and keep working just as hard as if the canter is true.

- The blue crosses on the short sides of the schooling area are important and, like the corners, must be ridden properly because they will let you know immediately if the quality of the canter is good enough and act as a guideline to check if he is working well enough – or not.

- It is immaterial where the cross is placed; somewhere near the middle of the short side will be fine, but it doesn't need to be exact, as much as 5ft or 6ft (1.5m or 1.8m) off-centre in either direction will work just as well.

- If the quality of the canter is good, the cross will be in the middle of the horse's stride. He will make his own adjustment off the corner because his hind leg will be strong and consistent enough to meet it spot on.

- The cross indicates whether or not you have ridden a good corner, and the good corner will produce the quality canter you are hoping for.

(Figures 7.2a and b, and 7.3a–c. See overleaf.)

Left and above **Figure 7.2a and b** You can see that Hannah and Willow are making a very good job of cross A as it is in the middle of their jump, showing that they have ridden into it from a good corner and produced the quality canter afterwards to get the perfect take-off at the next jump.

Don't cut corners!

As you approach any of the turns on the course, you must be aware early enough of trying to ride a slightly squarer route than normal. But don't *ever* think the horse is being naughty by cutting the corners; he will just be demonstrating that he knows where he is going and is happy to go there. He is using his brain and sometimes that will be very useful, but not in this context. It is up to you to thwart the horse from cutting in on the turn and so many riders underestimate how soon the horse is planning to do so.

The outside rein needs to be supporting him well before the corner, indeed immediately after landing from every jumping effort. The jumps and crosses will help you to practise how quickly you need to recover and rebalance after a jump if the quality of the canter is to be maintained (Figures 7.4a and b).

Incorrect canter leads and going disunited

There is a small but vital point to mention at this stage; if the horse is on the wrong lead or goes disunited what should you do? Should he be asked to trot and retake correct canter? *No!* Should you wriggle and shift your weight to try to encourage true canter? *No!*

- Just keep riding forward from the leg, nudging consistently to ensure he stays in canter, even if it's muddled.

- Maintain the feel with the outside rein, keep the inside shoulder up, and try to put more weight in the outside stirrup.

- However hard you find it to ignore a messy canter, you should keep going and allow him to rebalance and sort his own legs out.

Figures 7.4a and b a) Bertie certainly believes in an active canter but even a still photo shows that he has taken charge, slanting in before the corner, and is really going much too fast rather than working hard. More outside rein required *sooner* to steady and keep him out on the turn please Rosie!

b) That's more like it! Rosie's outside rein is engaged and supporting well before the turn, her inside shoulder is more level, and Bertie has a much stronger hind leg. He would be able to jump very nicely with this sort of canter.

Opposite page: far left and left
Figures 7.3a–c a and b) Sally and Skewiffy show a cracking canter leading to a very stylish jump. **c**) Izzie and Dougal meet the jump on a perfect and powerful take-off stride. Note the similarity of the two jumps from two very different animals.

- He will either change into true canter, or not. But he will be balanced enough if you prevent him leaning in. As long as one hind leg is actively working as he takes off, it doesn't have to be the one you prefer.

- It would obviously be smoother and more comfortable if the canter was true, but get over it! Just ride and allow him to do the job.

- He will have every opportunity to do that job if you give him the chance instead of protectively bringing him back to trot or circling.

EXERCISE 1

The foundation exercise

PURPOSE OF THE EXERCISE

Recognising and producing the power canter to make the jumping foolproof is the main point of the practice. The A and B blue cross poles at each end of the school help to develop squarer corners and the crosses, the grid and jumps – or ground poles – are there to confirm if you are getting it right. If you are, clear and clean jumping will be the result.

Check Diagram 1, see opposite; in addition to the blue crosses you will work over the small bounce grid and the two other small jumps around the outside of the school jumping area. This exercise should be ridden on both reins, always starting with the bounce grid of red crosses.

Green route = good route

Red route = bad route

I'm sure you're wondering just how hard it can be to ride round the outside of the school or practice area; well, I'd say from long experience it will be more difficult to get it right to start with than you might think!

Make your mind up to ride only the green route. If the red route starts to creep in, the canter will not be as effective and you will not be getting the good shot at the obstacles that the green route will encourage.

The blue crosses

The all-important A and B blue cross poles are set on the short sides of the jumping area. They will get the desired result if they are placed more or less in the centre of the short side although as much as 5ft or 6ft (1.5m or 1.8m) either way will be fine. Wherever they are, if the horse is working well, he should adjust from the corner to meet them comfortably.

The bounce grid of red crosses

As this exercise can be ridden in both directions, this grid should be set so that the crosses are identical in size so the helper can observe what is happening without constantly being distracted by changing the jumps round. (Figures 7.5a–d, see overleaf)

Grid distances

The distances between each grid element should be as follows.

- For a horse – 12ft (3.7m)

- Under 14.2hh – 11ft (3.4m)

- Under 13.2hh – 10ft (3m)

- Under 12.2hh – 9ft (2.7m)

The two jumps

Note that the two jumps on the long side of the school opposite the grid are also jumped from both directions and, like the grid, should be set accordingly. When you are riding on the right rein, these jumps are 11 and 15 and on the left rein, 3 and 7. If however you are just using poles, try to place them in the same position as the jumps suggested.

RIDING THE EXERCISE

- Start the exercise by riding over the grid in the middle of the long side. Just like the blue crosses it won't matter if the grid isn't dead centre, as much as 8ft to 10ft (2.4m to 3m) either way will be fine, you will still have plenty of room to establish and practise the good canter. Start on whichever rein you prefer and be very positive from the word go.

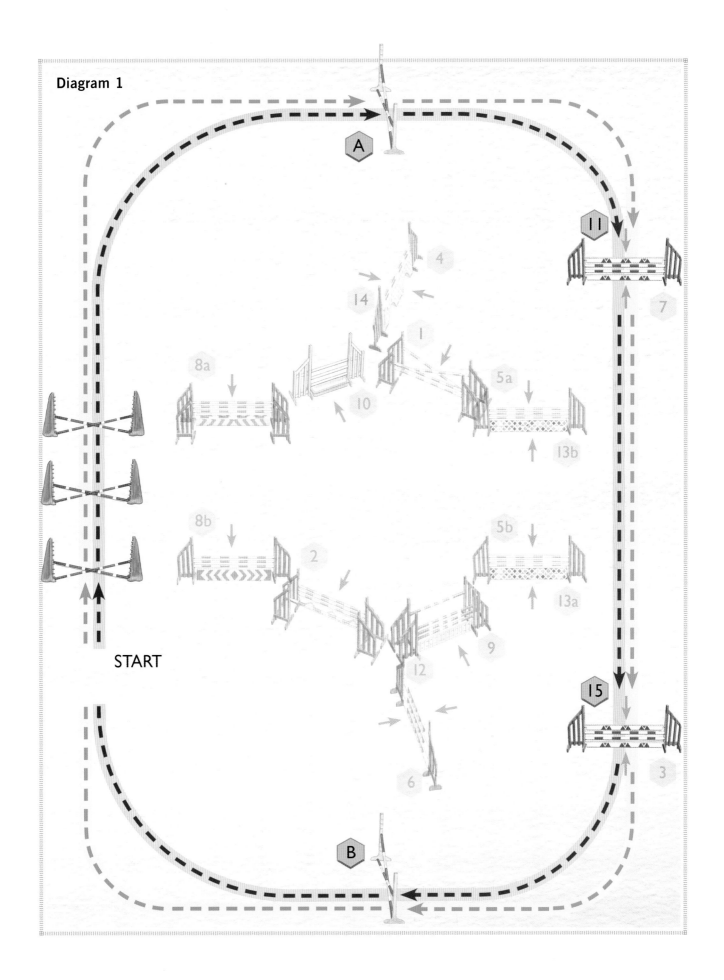

Diagram 1

Figures 7.5a–d Sally and Skewiffy have been very active through the grid and Sally has produced a good squarish corner to cross A as it is in the middle of her jump.

- As soon as you land, either from the grid, the crosses or the jumps, you should already be supporting your horse with the outside rein, and it's vital to recognize that steering round the approaching corner should not be the easy option of giving the outside hand. The inside hand must steer.
  - Outside rein for power, pace and energy.
  - Inside hand for steering.

- Keep your inside shoulder up as the corner gets nearer and your inside leg encouraging him to keep working into that supporting outside rein. *Don't* lean in and drop your weight more into the inside stirrup.

- Don't allow him to slant round the corner by letting up with the outside rein. Remember, he's

not being naughty; in his eyes he is just being rational in taking the quickest route, and it's up to you to hold him out.

- Visualise the corner being square.

- Try to ride that corner with a little more awareness of gathering the inside hind leg underneath him and encouraging him to stride strongly through underneath you instead of mincing round the turn.

- If you have produced a power corner, he should meet the crosses A and B on a good shot, wherever they are positioned on the short side, because the good corner will ensure he straightens up around the school with enough power and energy to sort his own stride out. This should be carried through to the grid and the jumps.

Remember, the two main benefits of the quality canter are that a horse will have enough impulsion to jump well, higher and wider when required, and he will meet the jumps far more often on a comfortable take-off point without the rider fussing and trying to adjust the stride by hooking or whooshing to the fence.

Watching the professionals

Study the top riders and their methods of jumping professionally. I always record Olympia or the Horse of the Year Show so that I can keep up to date with any little nuances that the very top riders use to maintain their performances.

It is most interesting to observe that occasionally a rider comes off a corner and starts riding like a dervish to the next fence instead of remaining cool and calm. On playback, you can see that the power on the corner has been allowed to relax and the rider needs to rapidly generate the revs again.

With the slight loss of oomph from the corner, they will usually manage a single fence successfully but if it's a short related distance, a double or combination, then the horse finds it hard to keep going strongly enough to cope.

Although the eventual knock-down or refusal may be well across the arena, the problem has started from the seemingly innocuous mistake made by the rider in allowing his attention to detail to slip in producing the good corner.

This doesn't have to happen, and the foolproof nature of this corner practice will give you as much awareness of what you should be doing as a top professional, it's how you keep it up that counts. The professional will usually be able to keep going automatically; it's when he doesn't that the errors creep in.

As mentioned earlier, you may feel that it can't be that hard to steer effectively round the ends of an arena but don't be misled; you *will* need to keep thinking about your technique and try hard all the way round the exercise to ride the corners as professionally as possible. Even more experienced riders fail to recognise how quickly the horse is planning his turn, and when training I am constantly shouting 'Out! Out! Out!' as soon as the horse lands, especially on the approach to a shorter corner. It is up to you, the rider, to be quick enough to prevent him cutting in, to hold him out and actually steer round the turns instead of letting him lean or collapse in (Figures 7.6a–c). It is also up to you to encourage the hind leg to keep pushing through round the corner,

Figures 7.6a–c Troy argues with Anna and she uses the corner and her outside rein to retrieve the better canter and contain the energy.

Figures 7.7a and b
Anna remembers how to keep this energy level up when Troy is asked to do something demanding. Her helper would have nothing to complain about here as she is looking up and producing a great take-off resulting in a very good jump.

to keep the energy level the same on the turns as on the straight (Figures 7.7a and b).

Do *not* try to organize the take-off point to the crosses, the grid or the two fences. Ignore their placement, don't look for it, and just keep riding with a supporting outside rein and an awareness of working hard to keep the canter consistent.

The better you ride the squarish corner in the right mode, gathering and pushing so the hind leg is strong and active, the better you will straighten up on full power and he will be ready and able for anything.

Summary

- This exercise gives you the opportunity to practise round four corners with four jumping efforts plus a small grid without repeating the jumps.

- If you need a breather, relax and take one. You won't achieve anything by doing the exercise again if you are getting puffed. It is hard work for you to make it easy for the horse.

- The more you practise, the more you will find that he is meeting his poles or jumps on a nice smooth take-off stride; the take-off and landing distance from the poles will become more equal. You don't need an expert to tell you that, and if you aren't sure if it's correct or not, look at your last set of footprints.

- Just remember that when you can see a 'good' stride coming you still need to keep riding and supporting, if you anticipate the take-off point and shoot your hands forward you will lose all that power that the well-ridden corner has given you.

- It is only a foolproof exercise if you keep working hard.

- As always, repeat the exercise on the other rein.

EXERCISE 2

Cross poles and simple figure-of-eight steering

PURPOSE OF THE EXERCISE

Once you've mastered the art of working round a corner on full power and you're finding your approaches and jumping easier and more successful you will be ready to add a bit more to the format. The whole object of this exercise is to put into practice the power canter and the preparation and presentation to ensure that your horse goes where you want him to.

Check Diagram 2, see opposite: you will work from blue cross A to jumps 11 and 12, to blue cross B, to jumps 3 and 4 and on to cross A again.

Green route = good route

Red route = bad route

RIDING THE EXERCISE

- Start on the right rein to cross A and continue round the corner, on a squarish line as with Exercise 1, and then straight to jump 11.

- After 11, ride straight along the fence with a supporting outside rein to keep the impulsion consistent, and steer with the inside rein to number 12. Ride an effective turn, not too early so don't anticipate and rush, and present your horse square on to number 12. You can see from the diagram that if you allow the red route to dominate and let him cut the corner to number 12, taking it on the slant or angle, you will have very little room to ride the sort of turn you need to the cross at B.

- It is vital that you keep your shoulders level and try very hard not to lean in because the result of

good steering is that he will take a straight line to cross B on full revs and meet it on a good shot. If he doesn't, the main reason will be that you've either allowed him to cut in early before 12 and jump across it, which is very easy with an upright (and with too much cut-in you will run out). Alternatively you might have eased the outside rein over the jump or immediately on landing and let him lean in on the corner. This is where your helper will be most valuable, as it will be very plain to see what's gone on. If your horse is set on cutting the corner to cross B, his hind leg will mince or even stutter and the cross will not be in the middle of his stride. He won't have the power, energy or time to sort his legs out for himself. (Figures 8.1a–c, see overleaf)

- You have practised this corner in Exercise 1 and so you have no excuse to cut in on the approach.

- Whether you get it right or not, keep going and think forward. Number 3 and the turn to number 4 will come up on you rather quickly even if your cross B has been spot on.

- Keep looking ahead as you need to be already planning the green route to number 4 and beyond to the turn to cross A (Figures 8.2a–f, see overleaf).

Steering and impulsion

If your steering and impulsion are good, you will sail round smoothly. If they're not, keep practicing until you do. It's a very basic skill to be able to steer, but

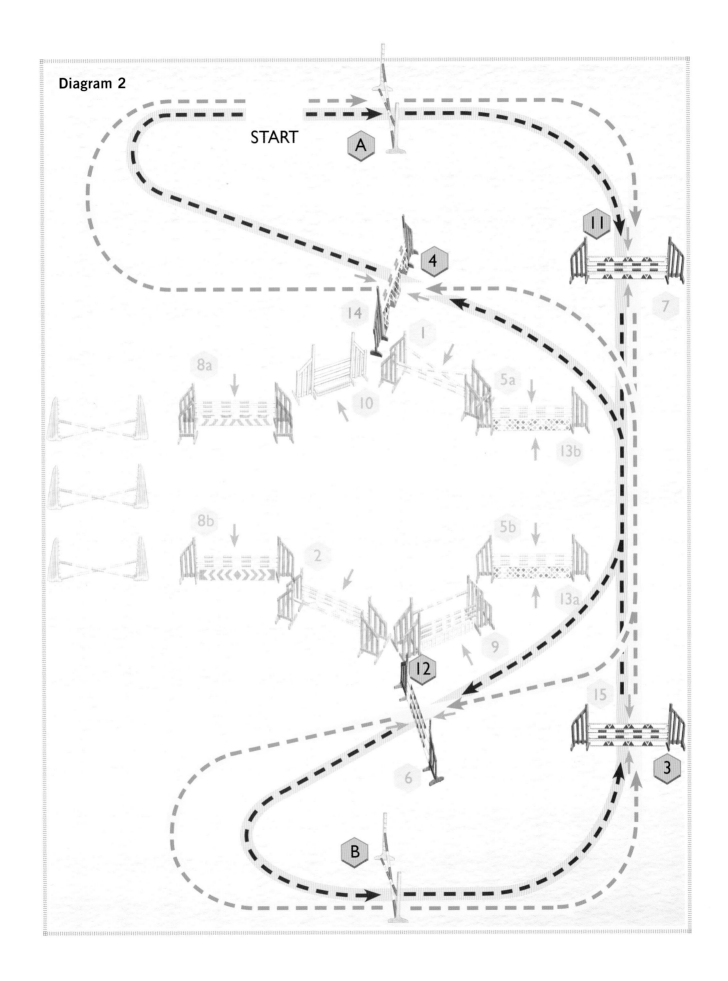

Diagram 2

START

Above **Figure 8.1a–c a**) Fergus has stolen the line round the corner to number 12 and is planning a too economical route to cross B, the red route. **b**) Cathy's right shoulder is as droopy as Fergus's right knee. **c**) Cathy's shoulders are all square again now, but she must mind the wing doesn't catch her knee as this determined and ambitious show-off wants to anticipate every turn and cut in on the red route every time.

you will need to be quick to read the situation and prevent mistakes creeping in.

Your helper will easily be able to see and point out if your lines are wrong and where you may be bulging out or cutting in. You don't need to be an expert to watch and assess to see if the horse is wiggling or not.

The jumps in themselves are very simple and should be set to be a sensible size; it's the presentation you want to get right. If you get to the jumps with the right sort of power it will be very easy for him to have a trouble-free take-off point without you over-organising or interfering other than to give him power and good steering.

Again, your helper will be able to tell you what they can see, so be prepared to listen if the exercise hasn't gone as smoothly as you hoped for. If you are getting too close or too far away to take off comfortably, or kicking poles out, have a go at

following their advice. Even if you think they are wrong, next time at the very least change your route, if only slightly.

Analyse your approaches

Don't keep doing the same things, work out what is different about your next approach to the exercise and decide if the result has been better, the same, or worse.

You will be able to analyse for yourself what works best and what doesn't by a little bit of trial and error ... just not too much error please. Certainly a decent trainer would pick up on the mistake quickly, but it shouldn't take you long to work out how to self-correct. You should have done enough work by now to recognise when he is working hard enough, which really only leaves the steering to be improved.

Bottom row, opposite page and below
Figures 8.2a–f a) Nice jump at number 4 but Guy is already planning to cut the corner round to the cross at A. **b)** He doesn't intend to give in easily, he wants to take the red route. **c)** But Anne won't give in either and it's a real tussle to keep him out for the next turn. **d)** Anne just about manages to hold him out on the corner to cross A. **e)** The quality canter leading to (**f**) the good shot to cross A.

My first suspicion would always be that your route was slightly wrong and you were allowing the horse to dictate the steering by cutting in; that's usually the problem.

There may be one or two very minor and subtle adjustments that the trainer might suggest to help, but probably nothing more than common-sense advice. You and your helper between you should manage to work it out practically, not necessarily trying to pull the solution from a vast depth of horse knowledge that you don't possess!

Don't let the fear of being wrong stop you trying again on your own. You're not going to hurt the horse if the jumps are effortlessly in both your comfort zones. You may not make it perfect, but it shouldn't be a disaster, just do the things you know are right, and jolly well look where you want to be going!

Accept some input from your helper. With a minimum of practice they will be able to see clearly what is going on and to encourage you with some very common-sense remarks.

8.3 Anne and Guy in perfect accord.

- If you cut the corners, 'Keep out' or 'Stay straight' will remind you to hold more outside rein.

- If your shoulder drops or 'leads' on the turns across to 12 and 4: 'Shoulder up', 'Look where you're going', 'Turn your head sooner', should do the trick.

- If you are looking down at the jumps, your helper will spot it: 'Chin up' or 'Stop peeking'.

- They can see the horse's inside hind leg on the turns; is it coming as far underneath his body as it does on the straight? If not, 'More leg, but no faster' is the call required.

- And the ultimate encouragement? 'Keep working.'

It doesn't have to be complicated, just make sure you are trying to follow the green route with lots of leg producing lots of impulsion into lots of consistent contact!

If possible, repeat the exercise two or three times without having a breather, you will find that it will be easier the more you do. The only thing you have to guard against is that your horse will start to anticipate the route and cut in, so you will need to remain absolutely reliable with the steering.

EXERCISE 3

Cross poles and more difficult figure-of-eight steering

PURPOSE OF THE EXERCISE

Exercise 3 will use the same crosses and jumps as Exercise 2, but the figure of eight will be reversed and all the jumps will be ridden in the opposite direction. This workout will be slightly more demanding than the previous one as the fence line or edge of the working area will not be so helpful to the turning required. You will have to make a more conscious effort to negotiate the turns involved without relying so much on the fence to help you as you square up to the diagonal obstacles.

Check Diagram 3, see opposite: you will work from blue cross A to jumps 14 and 15, to blue cross B, to jumps 6 and 7 and on to cross A again.

Green route = good route

Red route = bad route

RIDING THE EXERCISE

- Start on the left rein to cross A. It is absolutely vital to hold your horse straight as he lands otherwise you simply won't have room to ride the turn to number 14. The fence of the arena may be too far away to guide you round so you will have to make a positive choice about where you begin to turn: too early and too tight and you stand the risk of losing impulsion as the hind leg can't keep working through; too late and you will bulge and sprawl and have to re-steer as you complete the turn.

- Try very hard to jump 14 in the middle and land straight so that you can hold him across the school to prevent him diving round the corner too close to the double at number 5.

- If you let him cut in to run down the fence line to number 15 he will be on the forehand and losing impulsion all the way. Be very positive as you approach and exit number 15, trying to use the technique established in Exercise 1 as you jump cross B.

- Again, remember that the arena fence may be too far away to help you turn to number 6 and the same negative aspects of losing impulsion or bulging out will apply unless you guide the turn successfully.

- This is an excellent exercise to practise everything you've done so far. Hold your horse consistently into the outside rein for power and steer well enough as you make a positive dog-leg turn to straighten up for number 7. And don't be relieved to get there nicely and forget to hold out and work round the corner to cross A.

(Figures 9.1a and b, and 9.2, see overleaf)

If the exercise has been ridden well, by the time you get to this stage of the Foolproof work your horse should be meeting the jumps on a pretty comfortable take-off point. He should arrive there with impulsion and power and be sorting his own stride out.

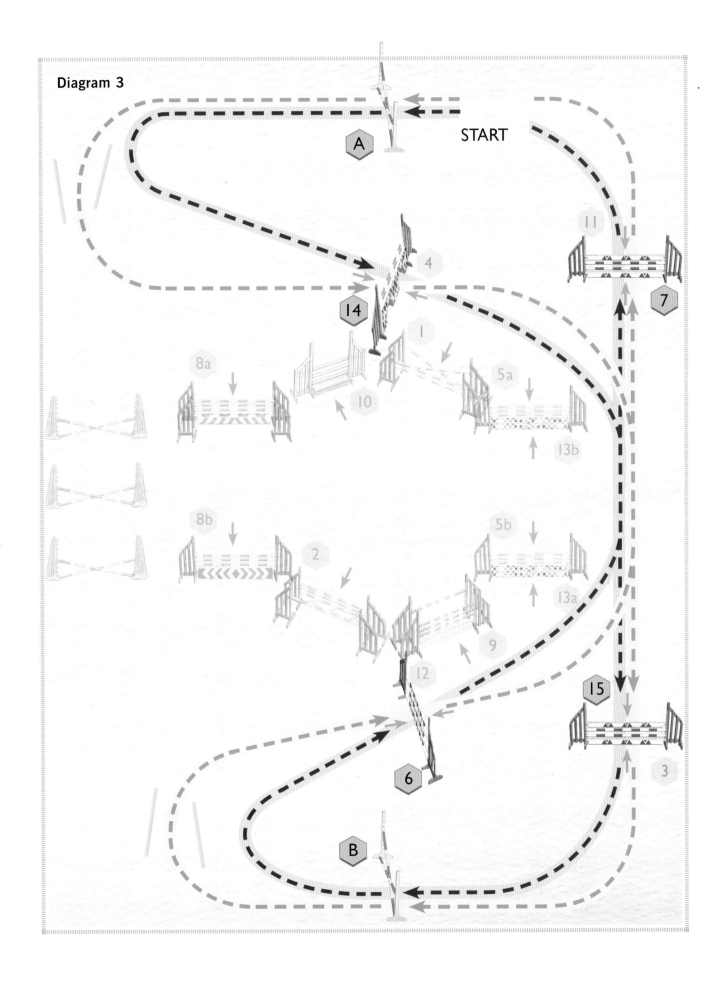

Diagram 3

START

Above **Figures 9.1a and b** There's no loss of impulsion or bulging as Willow flies across to number 6. Although she jumps it well, it is too fast and Hannah struggles to steady her down for number 7.

Right **Figure 9.2** The inevitable result of going too fast to number 7. The trouble started on the approach to number 6 and Hannah needs to take a stronger outside rein over the blue cross B and nag Willow to steady and cooperate round the turn and keep up that nagging all the way down on the long run to number 7.

You should have the confidence to keep pushing and gathering all his energy with a consistent contact.

If things don't go according to plan, you know the remedy by now. Have another go and don't try to insist on organising his jump. Organise his canter and change your route slightly and let him show you how well he can do.

Anticipation

Experience as a trainer has shown that the horse will mostly try to cut in, anticipate the next jump and want to get there more quickly than is advantageous but you must keep in mind that the horse is definitely not being naughty. He has a brain and he knows where he's going and he can't see the point of taking a wider route when he can get to the next jump more quickly. That's a great attitude to encourage in a jump-off when you're both good enough to have plenty of impulsion off a tight turn, but not so good when you're practising on your own and you keep knocking poles down unnecessarily.

It is not only the horse who anticipates either. Unless you focus your concentration on the correct route, you may inadvertently be giving your horse unconscious signals to cut in by a change of body-weight/position as you approach your turns.

Get your helper to stand head on to a jump, and it's usually the exit from the cross that is ridden badly; they will be able to tell you how quickly the horse is cutting in and how much further you need to be straight after landing.

Use a wiggle pole on the inside of the better route if you need a guide (see Diagram 3 for positioning of yellow wiggle ground poles). It will help you stay out straight after the crosses. It might also help to have another wiggle pole to the outside of the better route if you need some help to stop you bulging out to 14 and 6.

Don't get cross if you find this exercise is more difficult than you expected and you don't succeed immediately. It *is* hard to get it right, and the big advantage of practising it when you're on your own or without an experienced trainer is recognising the value of repetition.

Subtle and timely changes

- Don't make a major adjustment to your steering and speed; gently does it and be subtle with your changes.

- It is far better to use the wiggle poles to help both of you negotiate your turns and steering than to haul him about and lose impulsion when you try to look further ahead to plan where you're going.

- Don't feel the work is so difficult that you want to move on to something else. The foolproof nature of these exercises is that they are progressive. If you're finding them hard, back off and do a little more work on the previous task and get both of you going smoothly again.

- Don't set yourself a time limit to get it right, what's the hurry? If you skip a step you'll be sorry,

especially as Exercises 4 to 7 involve more of the course jumps, setting you up for negotiating a whole course, which is exactly what you want to do better in the first place.

- Don't ignore your helper, just because they may not be well versed in horses and jumping training, they are there to *help* and they're doing their best. If they have no preconceived ideas about jumping jumps, they are far more likely to give you a down-to-earth honest opinion about what they can actually see happening in front of them. They will be able to keep an eagle eye on you all the way round: every landing after every jump or grid, every corner and turn, and will be able to keep up their running commentary: 'Stay straight' over the crosses; 'Keep out' on all the turns; 'Look where you're going'; 'Shoulder up'. All the usual comments will apply, and don't forget the clincher: 'More leg, but no faster'. Try to keep going whatever happens, unless your helper has had to nip in and replace some poles and is still in the way. However much you're concentrating on what you're doing, don't run them down!

This work is definitely more demanding than the earlier exercises, so don't feel you are good enough to get it right immediately. Overnight success rarely happens with any sport, so why should jumping horses be an exception? Once you've made your mind up to stay calm and be persistent, there will inevitably be an improvement in the work.

It would be unwise to move on to Exercise 4 until you're pretty happy with this more demanding figure-of-eight work, and once you start progressing to jumping more of the course fences you will recognise and appreciate the earlier efforts.

EXERCISE 4

Cross poles plus course jumps 1, 2, 3 and 4

Just because you're trying to ride a course of jumps, don't be in a hurry. The exercises to incorporate the course jumps should be ridden one at a time, just adding in three or four jumps to the crosses. It will be hard for you to concentrate on riding a whole course on full power until you've had some dress rehearsals first.

PURPOSE OF THE EXERCISE

Now it's time to put into practice all that earlier preparation to improve your steering and impulsion and, therefore, your jumping. You are going to make a start on the course jumps as numbered.

Check Diagram 4, see opposite: you will work from the red grid, to the blue cross A, to jumps 1 and 2, to blue cross B, to jumps 3 and 4 and on to cross A again.

Green route = good route

Red route = bad route

RIDING THE EXERCISE

- Start with the grid on the right rein to get your impulsion in gear (Figures 10.1a and b, 10.2a and b and 10.3).

- Once you've got the grid right, carry on over cross A, and then ride a pushy and consistent three-quarter turn to numbers 1 and 2.
  - So far you've only done square turns from cross A to number 11 and you've had the fence line to help you. Now you've got to do a bit more with the steering while still keeping the quality canter and you have to recognise that he will

Figures 10.1 and b First time into the red grid Alwin is fairly casual; second time round over the same jump he is much smarter and more active after the rehearsal.

Diagram 4

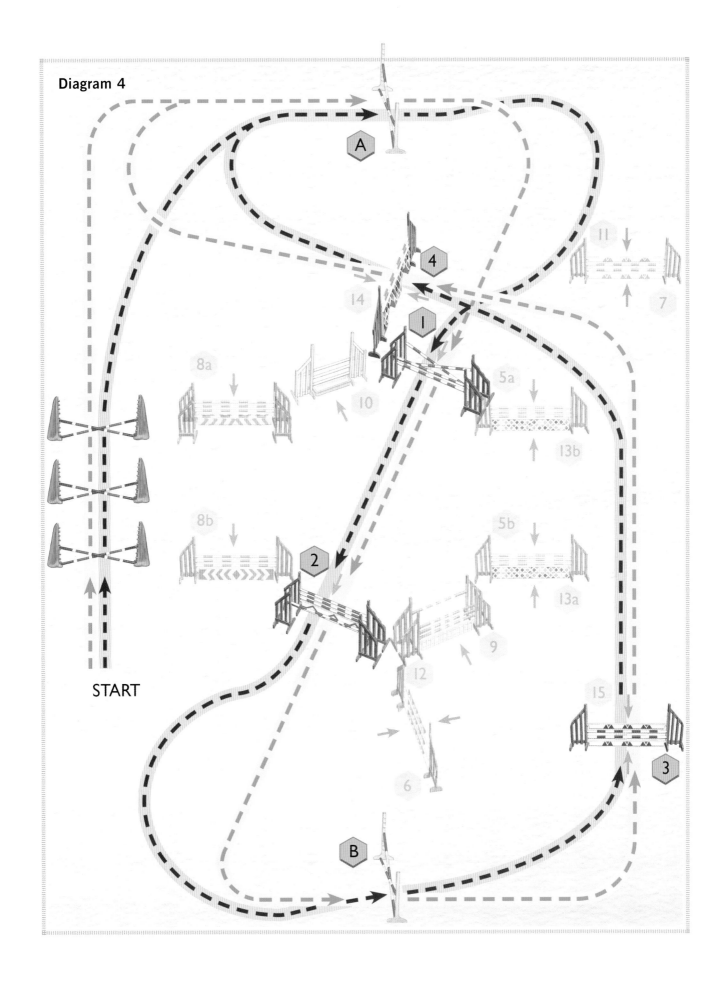

START

Above **Figures 10.2a and b**
Pippa now has the right
idea and has balanced
Alwin beautifully through
the grid, and his hind legs
couldn't be pushier; such a
good kick off to Exercise 4.

Right **Figure 10.3** Pippa
ventures on to the grass
course to put her work
into practice away from
the security of the arena;
she has learned it's best to
look up with a consistent
leg and contact. Practice
makes perfect (well,
effective anyway)!

not be expecting to do anything other than pop over number 11. He will be taken completely by surprise unless you are very positive in riding round the three-quarter corner.

- Turn your head and have tunnel vision to the jumps and steer soon enough so you should be square on to both numbers 1 and 2. (Figures 10.4a–e)

- Don't give your outside rein away to help you round the corner as you will also be giving away your power. And you will bulge out and then have to correct your steering. Your helper will recognize immediately if you have ridden the wrong route, and of course, so will you as you aren't facing up to the jump with the right sort of energy.

- The bulge gives the horse a bit of leeway to ease up on working so hard and he will take

Figures 10.4a–e a) Gaynor and Storm are absolutely square through the grid ready to start the course. **b)** A super jump at number 1 with Storm looking eager to go across to number 2. **c)** Gaynor is trying hard to be very level so that Storm lands in true lead. **d)** Gaynor is a bit forward a bit soon but (**e**) nice and level giving Storm every chance to take correct canter as he knows he will be turning left towards 3.

that opportunity to do so. With the resulting loss of impulsion the effectiveness of the jump is compromised.

- You will be far more successful if you turn a little earlier after the cross than you think you need to. If you've turned a bit too early, it's easy enough to slightly widen the approach to be square to number 1.
- If you get too wide and bulge you actually have to ride a change of direction, and it's never good to have a wiggly line to the first fence.
- I often use wiggle poles on the ground to help the rider appreciate how much they need

to be in charge after landing to ride a three-quarter turn from the cross to get a straight approach to the next jump. Your confidence and power will be so much more consistent if you have a bit of help to steer better. Use a wiggle pole where you need it, probably on the outside of the turn to number 1, to prevent you bulging until you are sure you can manage the successful turn without it (Figures 10.5a and b).

- Once you have mastered the three-quarter turn and riding straight to number 1, you will then be in a good position to ride the straight line across

Figures 10.5a and b a) Sue makes sure of riding a power corner to number 1 with strategically placed wiggle poles. She is very straight to the jump but right of centre. She needs to judge the steering from her corner a little more confidently and not turn quite so early. **b)** She also uses a wiggle pole after number 2 to guide them out to get a good turn to cross B and, although still right of centre, she has held the good straight line across the distance.

to number 2. It is a related distance of three non-jumping strides and you should be able to sail across on three and meet it comfortably whether your horse is long or short striding, as long as you keep the energy level of the canter up. If he puts in an extra stride, as long as you ride that stride, he will still be able to jump just as cleanly.

- Don't try to dictate the take-off, just let him sort it for himself from a strong canter. If you stop riding consistently he will find it hard, and that's when the serious problems like refusals start to creep in.

- As discussed in The Foolproof Pony Plan ponies are generally very clever and because they have a shorter stride they will cope with whatever the distance is as long as they are ridden.

- The success of the striding and jumping on this related distance is conditional on the way you have ridden the 'in' corner to cross A and the 'out' corner away from it.

- If you have encouraged the horse to work as hard on the turns as you have when practising the earlier exercises, he will approach number 1 on full revs, you will keep him motivated from the corner and you will get the good shot to both 1 and 2.
  - If you get to number 1 lacking energy and make a poor effort, the diagram and your own common sense will show you how you've let the quality of the canter slide. You have either misjudged and bulged out or given the outside rein away to help the steering. Or both!
  - It is absolutely vital that you don't give up if your take-off points are not where you would like them to be. All the work you've done so far is to make it easy for him to get to the other side of a jump from a ridden stride. He won't care where he takes off as long as you ride him and he finds the effort easy.

- Use lots of leg into a supporting contact and he should manage to clear the jumps with no problems, even if it's not as comfortable or as 'perfect' as you want, settle for effective.
- Your helper should keep the wiggle poles in place until you are sure you can do without them, and you mustn't get hyped up. Just do the right things that you've been doing to get to this point. Work him round every corner and don't relax your aids.

- When you land after number 2, stay very supportive with your new outside rein and try not to ease it forward to help your turn. Steer positively with your inside hand so you ride to the next three-quarter turn (left-handed) to cross B without bulging out at that end either. Use a wiggle pole if necessary!

- After cross B it should be simple to ride the turn to number 3, you've already done that correctly in earlier exercises. If you cut in, you will meet it badly; if you hold out and work hard you will help him to be spot on. You and your helper will know if you've done well or badly! And if the latter, do what needs doing to correct it next time: *don't* cut in.

- Now check the turn to number 4, it's only what you were practising previously in Exercise 2. If you cut the corner (look at the diagram) you will get a rubbish turn to cross A because you won't have given yourself enough room to keep the hind leg pushing. Give him a touch more space to keep moving strongly (Figures 10.6a–e, see overleaf).

- If you get it wrong, when you mean to carry on round the course, the shorter turn after cross A to the double at number 5 will be extremely difficult to negotiate. So get it right now.

Figures 10.6a–e a) Bertie is a big young horse and needs all these exercises to give him confidence. This is a great corner to number 4; no cutting in here. **b)** Keeping that hind leg working. **c)** And look at the power. **d)** He's extravagant because he can be. **e)** Vicky has to work so hard to contain him and keep him active, but it's so worth the effort.

Opposite **10.7** Gaynor and Storm entirely focused on looking where they're going next.

EXERCISE 5

Cross poles plus course jumps 5, 6, 7 and 8

PURPOSE OF THE EXERCISE

Exercise 5 is suggested to help you to produce a good turn after blue cross A in order to be straight to the double at 5a and 5b; concentrating on a good dog-leg turn from 6 to 7; and another good turn after cross A to come straight to 8a and 8b.

Check Diagram 5, see opposite: you will work from the red grid, to blue cross A, to jumps 5a and 5b, to blue cross B, to jumps 6 and 7, to blue cross A, to jumps 8a and 8b, to cross B.

Green route = good route

Red route = bad route

This exercise is going to relentlessly test your response and steering as the approach to both doubles needs to be *straight*, no bulging out or cutting in after the cross A. Your reaction to take charge *immediately* you land from the cross must be rapid and impeccable in the execution; prepare and present with a vengeance!

Straight through a double

It is always wise to be straight through a double, any slight misunderstanding with the steering and it may actively encourage the horse to run out. If this happens, you will know why you have got it wrong and exactly what to do to correct it next time.

Remember how a simple turn badly executed will cause you grief. Anyone can steer a good corner with no pressure, but consistently doing so when there is

a course of jumps involved is not so easy. This is why the clarity and simplicity of improving the route and the impulsion is so uncomplicated to analyse. If you do it wrong, you will not get a good approach, if you do it right, the course will be straightforward and easy for your horse.

As you are now progressing with the course jumps, don't start to view the crosses as a nuisance; they are still there to remind you how vital it is to keep working consistently all the way round, and your helper will be able to step in to help reinforce what is required to do just that.

RIDING THE EXERCISE

- Start with the red grid on right rein, then the cross at A, but be prepared to visualise, and ask for, a square turn far sooner after the cross than you have before – and sooner than your horse is expecting – so that you get a nice straight approach to the double at 5a and 5b.
  - Be very positive with your steering hand while trying not to ease the outside rein to help you turn, and do keep pushing. The gridwork will help you recognize the impulsion needed through the double, and if you've ridden a nice straight line to it, there should be no problem with the distance for a nice one non-jumping stride.
  - If you allow your horse to angle across the middle of the double it will make the distance a touch longer as well as encouraging run-outs, so be square. Have your helper stand centrally behind you or head on to watch as

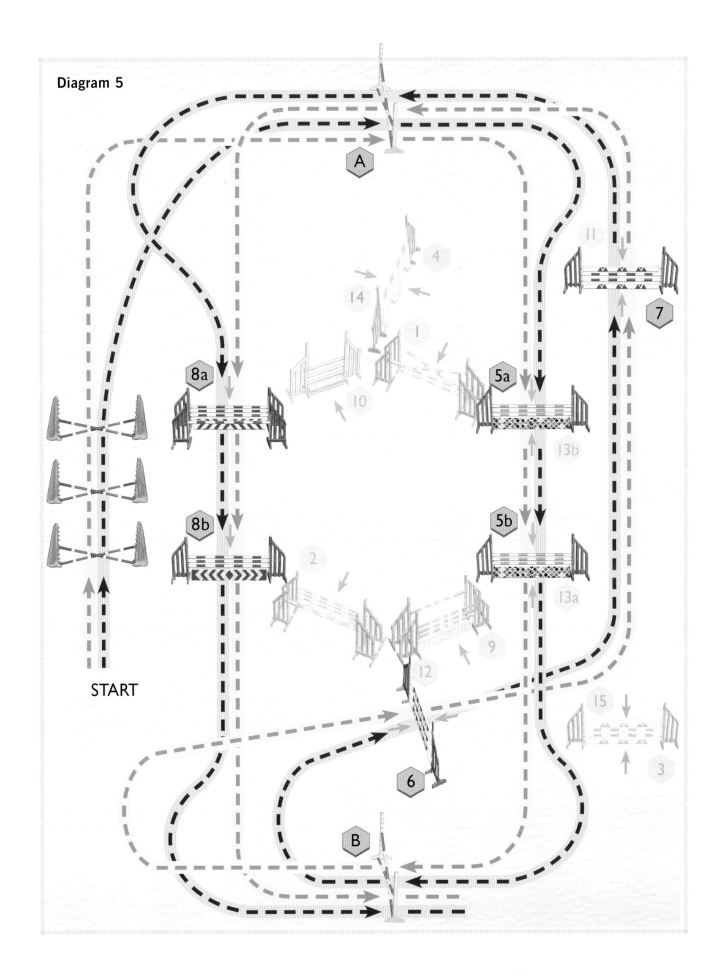

Diagram 5

START

Figure 11.1a–f Hannah and Bastion are absolutely straight going in to the double at number 5a, hold their line through the middle and they are spot on jumping out of the double at number 5b.

you approach 5a. As a trainer it is something I will often do as it's so plain to see if the double is ridden in a straight line or not and your helper will be able to see the same. If you are the helper, make sure you don't get in the way and be accused of putting the horse off if the exercise isn't successful. (Figure 11.1a–f)

- After the double, try not to bulge out. If you ride a straight line to the end of the school and go far enough down to execute a squarish turn to cross B you will be able to ride a power corner round to number 6. You've done this turn before, but not with the shorter approach to cross B which will make it a little more demanding. Don't slant to the cross and don't jump it pointing on an angle towards the fence.
  - Go a little bit further in the straight line than you think you need to so you can ride a better turn, even if you haven't too much straightening up room.
  - Giving the outside rein away to help you steer round the turn will result in a less than powerful approach to number 6, which again could result in a messy jump and a poor getaway to number 7.

- After number 6, keep the steering controlled and hold him out far enough so that you can ride a nice dog-leg turn and keep the energy gathered all the way to number 7 and beyond. This is only a repeat of part of Exercise 3 so you should be feeling pretty confident.

- Use lots of outside rein as you land after number 7 as you need to be straight after cross A because the approach to the double 8a and b requires the same square 'sooner' turn that you had to produce earlier in the exercise to 5a and b, i.e. prepare to visualise and ask for a square turn earlier after the cross than your horse will be expecting. You need to give him a nice straight line through the double (Figures 11.2a–e, see overleaf).

- Because there's more room left on this side of the school to allow for the grid, it will encourage both of you to drift wider on the approach. Don't be shy about using a wiggle pole at right angles to the end of the school if it helps you turn and straighten up more easily. It will give you the chance to practise what you tried to do at number 5a and b on the opposite rein. And it will also give you the chance to practise a straight line after the double and a non-bulging turn to cross B.

- Whatever you do, *don't* relax after number 8 and just allow the horse to collapse from his working mode round the corner to cross B, just because it's the last bit of the exercise.
  - It would be so disappointing if you did that at a show and had the last fence down because you relaxed too soon. One of the extra benefits of using the crosses at the end is to let you know just how long you need to keep going on full power. It is so sad and unnecessary for you to turn into a 'last fence jockey' and kick out the last pole because you thought you were home and dry.
  - The secret, as always, is to ride decent supported turns and try very hard to keep working in the consistent rhythm you know will work. That hind leg needs to be pushing strongly round the corner, not mincing on the spot. Your helper will immediately be able to see if you have cut the corner, so do be prepared to listen. It can't be emphasised enough that it's only a common-sense observation to put you in your place if the line has been ridden badly.

Repetition is the key to the success of the whole exercise. If you get it right the first time it may well be a fluke instead of the result of excellent riding. The horse will be slightly surprised by a new approach and be willing to listen and cooperate. It will be the second time when he knows where he's going that he will try to cut the corner more and it's up to you to insist that he goes where you want. He doesn't know that if he cuts the corner and doesn't work so hard, the slight lessening of impulsion will mean that his next jump won't be so easy. But you do, so make sure you do something about it!

Figure 11.2a–e Great jump from Poppy but you can see that although Rebecca is trying to keep straight through the double at 8, her weight has crept down a bit more into her right stirrup with predictable results: Poppy runs out.

11.3 Hannah and Bastion pinging the planks in great style.

EXERCISE **6**

Cross poles plus course jumps 9, 10, 11 and 12

PURPOSE OF THE EXERCISE

Exercise 6 will give you more practice keeping your horse straight and introduces the narrow jump 9 and narrower jump 10, which will make you concentrate on steering.

Check Diagram 6, see opposite: you will work from the red grid, to blue cross B, to jumps 9 and 10, to blue cross A, to jumps 11 and 12, to blue cross B.

Green route = good route

Red route = bad route

When you jump the course as a complete work-out, you will have ridden away from number 8, hopefully in a straight line to a square corner to cross B.

RIDING THE EXERCISE

Start with the grid on the left rein first, then cross B, and then plan your turn on the diagonal to numbers 9 and 10. Make sure you don't cut the corner; you might be surprised at how far across the school after cross B you need to go to ride the straight line to 9 and 10 (Figures 12.1a–c and 12.2a–d).

- Jump 9 is narrow in comparison to the other jumps. Jump 10 is even narrower with the possibility your horse will spook at the water tray, so make sure that your steering is deadly accurate. Use lots of leg as you straighten up to help you maintain the steering. You neither want to cut in to 10 early, nor bulge out on the approach.

- If you're not sure of getting it right first time, use wiggle poles. You and your observer will already know if your horse has a tendency to cut in or

bulge out, so get your helper to put the wiggle pole down in the most useful spot.

- If he tends to cut in, put the pole where he has to go round it to help you hold him out.
- If he prefers to bulge and curl round your leg, place the pole so he has to go inside it to encourage you to keep him in line a bit sooner.

- Look well ahead to number 10 and, again, make sure you're very secure with your steering; as the jump is so narrow you only have to waver slightly across the school to actively encourage him to run out.
- Ask your helper to move behind you as you turn so that they can see immediately if and where you start to deviate from the straight line across the diagonal. Usually it will be as soon as you've landed from the first fence (in this case 9) in the line, but not always.
- Your helper will be able to spot immediately if you have dropped your weight to one side and affected the steering, by checking if your shoulders stay level.

- As soon as you've landed after 9, concentrate particularly on the quality canter. The next jump is even narrower and has a water tray to contend with as well. Be ready to use more leg to keep him going forward in case he doesn't like the look of it and make sure your steering is accurate too. It would be very easy for him to try to run out and for you to allow it to happen if you don't switch your attitude to amber alert.

- As long as the water tray has caused no spooky problems it should be a nice straightforward turn to cross A. Just make sure that you aren't cutting

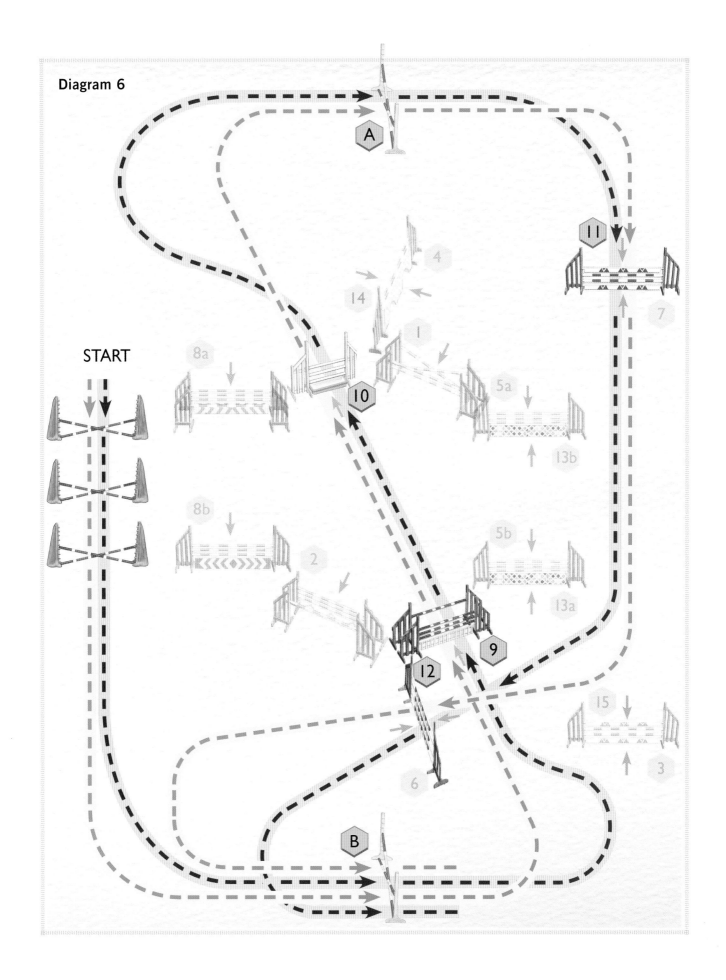

Diagram 6

START

Figures 12.1a–c a) India has ridden a good turn to number 9 on Flint and even in the air has tunnel vision to the middle of number 10. **b)** On landing she tries hard to collect and steady Flint and manages just in time to produce the good canter and (**c**) a good jump at number 10.

Figure 12.2a–d
a) No problems for Isobel and the young Maybe at the water tray in the arena, but it's a very different challenge out on the grass. b) The tray obviously looks very different to her without the security of an enclosed arena. c) Isobel is very committed, even if slightly precarious. d) Just come again, practice makes perfect (or at least effective). But just to remind you that horses are not machines, Isobel couldn't even get a canter to start with, let alone a quality one, on the grass approach. Maybe required a few hefty encouraging kicks to get going!

in and go far enough towards the fence line before asking him to turn so that you don't lose any power by allowing the hind leg to be a touch lazy.

- As you head for numbers 11 and 12 it would be easy to be complacent because they are the slightly easier options on this twisty route but make no mistakes. If you relax and allow him to cut the last corners to 11 and 12 because of the familiarity of these two jumps it will be very easy to lose power and concentration. It will be so disappointing to have ridden the narrower obstacles well and then rattle the odd pole because you haven't kept up the consistency of the power canter.

- Remember to make the good turn and jump cross B to complete the exercise and don't just collapse too soon with relief at having done well.

  - However hard you are concentrating on steering round parts of the course, you must keep that hind leg coming through on the turns to maintain that high-quality jumping canter. Your helper should be on your case and reminding you to keep working hard too.

EXERCISE 7

Cross poles plus course jumps 13, 14 and 15

PURPOSE OF THE EXERCISE

Remember how you had to do a fairly smart turn on the right rein to get straight to the double at 5a and b? Exercise 7 enables you to practise the similar turn to the double the other way, from the left rein, and jumps 13, 14 and 15 complete the course.

Check Diagram 7, see opposite: you will work from the red grid, to blue cross B, to jumps 13a and 13b, to blue cross A, to jumps 14 and 15, to blue cross B.

Green route = good route

Red route = bad route

RIDING THE EXERCISE

• Start by popping through the grid on the left rein.

• Ride straight down the school to make the squarish turn to cross B. This should be getting almost automatic by now so don't start to relax, you need to be very positive for the shortish turn out to approach 13 accurately.

• Don't make a slanted turn; use a wiggle pole if you need it, and don't ignore your helper nagging you to stay straight on the longish run up to 13.

(Figures 13.1a–c)

• You have already practised the turn from the cross A to number 14 in Exercise 3, but it is one of the more difficult early exercises so don't relax, especially if you have just had a tussle at the preceding double.

• Don't relax on the longer approach to number 15 and the turn to cross B, there is no room for complacency with Foolproof exercises.

Figure 13.1a–c a) You can see from the position of the division in the wall fillers that Bertie has jumped well in the middle at the first part of the double at 13a but (**b**) is already making his intentions clear as he determinedly leans in to his left of centre and (**c**) exits over 13b well to his left. Rosie must keep her outside rein more secure as he is not going to get enough room on his next corner to keep up the good canter. Don't forget your landing stride is the beginning of the approach to the next jump, however far away it may be, and you don't want to allow the good canter to be squandered.

Diagram 7

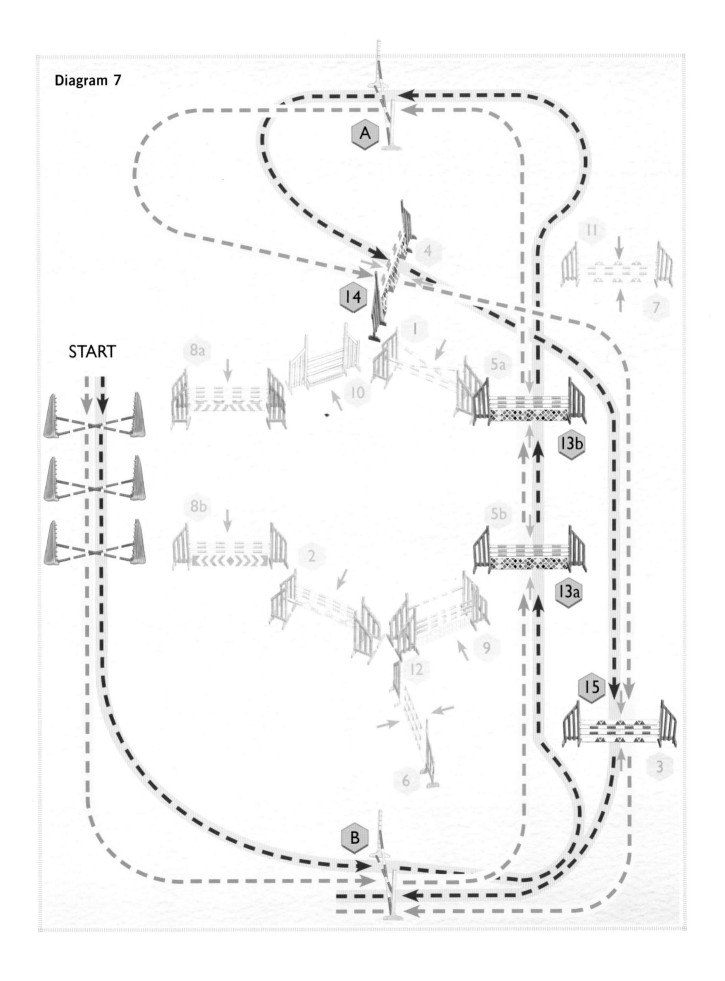

Conclusion and summary of Exercises 1–7

Conclusion

It will be hard to keep up the attitude required to continue to ride the canter well when you string all the work you have done in Exercises 1–7 together to try to ride the whole course.

- Do without the bounce grid and try to do without the wiggle poles, but retain the use of the crosses A and B each time you get to the ends of the school. They will help you keep reaffirming that all your corners are ridden on full power without cutting in and slanting to your next line of jumps.

- Your helper must now take full responsibility for nagging, bullying, cajoling, persuading, convincing or goading you into being consistent all the way round. If they see that you are getting puffed and the horse is suffering a loss of power as a consequence, they should step in and ask you to pull up. They will know this is happening by the simple observation that you are cutting corners, missing strides, and rattling poles.
  - Don't be negative if you have to have a breather, it would be disappointing to carry on and do badly when the only real problem would be a slight loss of strength and consistency, and don't argue because you feel taking that breather is a sad reflection on your riding ability. The practice course is long and demanding and very difficult to ride accurately; it's not designed to be easy. The actual length of the whole course is problematical enough without the turns and angles required to be consistently energetic and clean jumping. Eighteen jumping efforts without the addition of the crosses are more than enough.

- Initially I would suggest going from number 1 to as far as number 7 and cross A and then having a breather.

- When you're ready, restart by taking left rein and steering through the middle of the elements of the double at 5, try to stay parallel with both the jumps, so you can make a good left turn back on track to number 7, and carry on round the rest of the course as far as you manage to keep riding well.

- Don't feel it's defeatist if you don't get as far as 15 (not forgetting to finish over cross B) in one go, it would be sensible to rest if you find it hard to keep your own energy level up.

Summary

- Remember that the practice course suggested in these exercises is just that: a course I've built to give riders the opportunity to practise most options.

- If you can maintain the good canter that the earlier work has encouraged your horse should stay cooperative and listen to what you want him to do. But this won't always happen: when you are going well it is easy to relax, and when you do he will look over his shoulder and nab you!

- There is an opportunity with this course to pick and choose the exercises you feel you most need; they are only suggestions, but suggestions which will help you ride far more consistently and successfully to each jump.

- It won't matter a bit if you hire someone else's arena/school or try to build as much or as little at home as you can manage. Just try to put strategic crosses at each end of your practice area to ensure that they will help you re-establish the quality of the canter as you ride your turns. And have a few wiggle poles at the ready.

- Don't make light of your practice when you use a few ground poles placed in the position of all or some of the course jumps; it is still very valuable practice and the poles are no less significant just because they aren't jumps.

- It is producing the quality of the canter that's so important, and then maintaining that quality canter while allowing the poles and crosses to let you know if you can keep that canter workmanlike.

- It will be so easy for your helper to see if these substitute jumps are in the middle of the horse's stride as he goes over them and they must tell you and remind you to keep working. You don't need 'posh' kit to practise that, or an experienced trainer; your long-suffering helper will be more than adequate to encourage, support and criticise you.

- If, however, you are finding that you've reached an impasse with your efforts, then it will be time to enlist the help of a lesson with an experienced trainer. Try to take your helper to the lesson; they may not be able to pick up the finer points of the methods used to set you on the right track, but if the trainer is genuinely interested in helping you, then your helper should be given some valuable pointers to remind you how to ride more effectively in between sessions.

- You can only organise so much professional help: financial restrictions, travel and work often get in the way of training as much as you would wish and that is perfectly understandable. But there's no reason why you shouldn't manage to not only maintain the status quo between lessons but also, with the assistance of your helper plus the Foolproof exercises suggested, actually increase your ability to improve.

EXERCISE 8

Pat 'n' push grid

PURPOSE OF THE EXERCISE

The pat 'n' push exercise is about improving your timing. Your weight needs to be in the right place at the right time and the contact needs to be just right to lighten the horse's front end to pat the ground and enable him to get the strong push up, the vital ingredient, from the back legs. It is a great work-out for:

- producing a strong take-off

- recognising why you are knocking poles down

- most significantly, how to do something about it.

The pat 'n' push exercise is so called because I envisage the horse touching down, 'patting' the ground with his front legs in between the bounce jumps, and then 'pushing' upwards strongly with his hind legs.

A simple bounce combination used with the right mental approach will vastly improve the way you both jump.

Check Diagram 8, see opposite: look at the hoof prints; they show the position of the horse's **back feet** prior to take off. If you don't collect or gather the horse's stride well enough as he jumps in to the bounce, the hind feet when they touch down between the elements will be wide apart and have nowhere near enough power or 'push' to spring smartly and cleanly over the next jump.

Green route = good hoof prints

Red route = bad hoof prints

So, having completed Exercises 1–7 you've got the good canter, your horse is meeting nearly all your obstacles on a good stride, but it's not quite enough to stay jumping cleanly. Why are you rattling poles in front, behind or with all four feet and how can you sort it out?

Try this very simple pat 'n' push exercise. Just canter over two crosses or small jumps on a bounce distance? How easy is that?

It is, however, very easy to be sloppy, slovenly and casual! It's your *attitude* to *how* you use those two crosses that matters so much and you will certainly need to have your helper there resetting the poles and watching your efforts to see what is happening. You are going to rattle them mightily until you both get the hang of this work-out. The rider rides and the helper observes: a concerted effort between you will rapidly make an improvement to the horse or rider who may be a little casual or careless with poles. The actual position of the front feet as you land for the 'pat' is not the most important component of the exercise. (Figures 15.1a–f)

It is the power and energy produced by the push that you must strive for, and of course it's so simple for your helper to watch those back feet to see if they are close or wide. The closer they are together in the middle of the bounce, the more vertical the jump will be, the better chance of jumping cleanly.

I have just been watching a top international six-bar competition where there are five or six jumps in a straight line increasing in size with two strides between each one. It is a great opportunity to observe the experts in full flight and so easy to spot the ones who are going to clear the jumps cleanly. They are the

Diagram 8

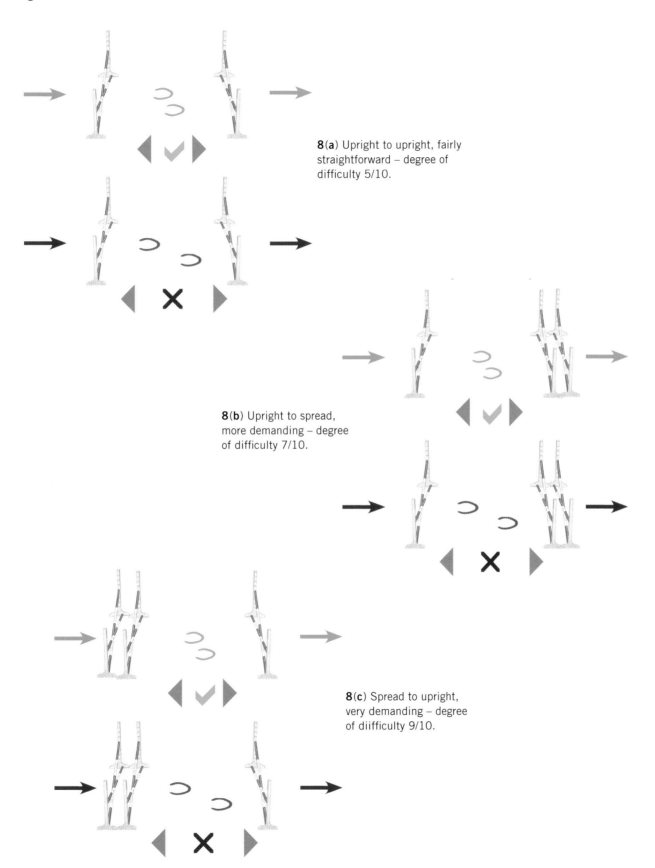

8(a) Upright to upright, fairly straightforward – degree of difficulty 5/10.

8(b) Upright to spread, more demanding – degree of difficulty 7/10.

8(c) Spread to upright, very demanding – degree of diifficulty 9/10.

horses whose riders are keeping hold, not tipping forward to the jumps, and those horses' back feet are pushing off the floor almost together.

The rider's contribution to the success of the exercise

Understanding the exercise

Understanding what you are hoping to encourage the horse to do must be very plain to you, your horse and your helper. The horse needs to be ridden so effectively and consistently that it is easy for him to clear the jumps without knock-downs. He needs to be helped to get a more vertical take-off to complete the exercise successfully and his energy needs to be directed 'up' instead of 'along'.

The work will not only help him jump cleanly in the controlled conditions of the practice area, it will improve his technique and, most particularly, your timing and balance in the air. It won't harm your steering efforts either.

If the angle of the crosses is fairly sharp, even though the jump may not be high, he will only need to be a few inches off-centre and the poles will rattle,

Figures 15.1a–f Ben's canter is strong and although he is a little further away from the first cross than ideal Sarah has a very supportive contact and plenty of leg. He jumps in confidently and although he doesn't land ideally in the middle of the distance, it's irrelevant as his 'push' is perfect enabling him to jump whatever comes next beautifully. Note how his front legs are folded smartly over the jump, no dangling. Don't forget, when you're jumping round a course, however good the canter is, you are unlikely to meet every jump at the perfect take-off point, it's how you ride the stride that you have which will ensure a good jump. You must 'pat 'n' push'.

not necessarily because he is being careless, but just because he will be gauging the height of the jump by the middle or lowest point of the cross. If he jumps it off-centre, therefore, it will immediately be a few inches higher than he expected.

Repetition will ensure that you have lots of practice in producing the horse's 'jump' without any stress. The secret of improvement is to just keep coming again, trying hard to produce the nice strong bouncy canter which will help the horse's lift-off.

Listen to your helper. If the horse is not improving, there are lots of phrases your helper can offer, and either one or several of them will help. It is a question of recognising what slight change from you makes the big change in the horse's technique. With a concentrated two-effort exercise any little nuance or change will make a difference, and once you discover which slight change makes an improvement, log it in

to your memory for future reference when the same mistakes start to creep in again. Helpers will soon learn that their riders are notoriously repetitive with their bad habits.

Leave the horse alone

It would be very easy to get it wrong and have the horse kick the poles out because you are trying to help him to jump rather than work harder. You must try to resist the temptation to hook the horse back, or whoosh the horse forward, to what you perceive to be the perfect take-off point.

If the canter is the right sort of canter for jumping, and we have already seen how important that canter is by using the cross poles at the two ends of the arena, then the horse will more and more often get to the first cross on a good shot. He will sort it out himself from a position of strength in his stride rather than a continually interfering rider.

It is very difficult for you to be facing even a small cross pole thinking you are going to be too far off or too deep, especially if you have been knocking poles down. It is so tempting to try to boss the horse in to taking off where you prefer. But you must resist, resist!

At some point his hind-leg power will begin to improve because you will be producing enough impulsion and balancing and maintaining that power. It will be easier for him to meet the jumps comfortably and jump cleanly. The only difference to your rate of progress for this particular exercise is the time it takes for that improvement to be established and dependable.

The exercise is very simple so try hard to practise it at every opportunity, not just under strict supervision; it's so very basic, you shouldn't go far wrong. And if you don't get it right immediately, the work is not so complicated that he will lose confidence in you. Another few tries with the right attitude should sort things out. The helper's observations, hopefully accurate even if inexpert, will also make such a difference to your confidence in yourself and your horse.

Constructive criticism of the horse

Any rattling of the poles – in front, behind, first cross or exit fence – *must* be criticized. Unless your horse understands that you are a bit cross when he rattles a pole, he won't bother to try too hard. Why should he? If nobody tells him off for having a casual attitude, he won't much care whether he is pleasing you or not if you grin and bear it and say nothing. So make sure there is a grumble, a hiss, or a loud 'Oi' if he touches a pole. If he doesn't much care about a verbal grumble, the ideal alternative is a short jumping stick with a flappy-slappy split end. If you tap your leg, boot or saddle with this it will, again, reinforce his understanding that touching a pole is naughty. The noise and implied warning will work wonders.

The shortness of the exercise will give you the opportunity to tell the horse off immediately if he is careless. This criticism must not be omitted, even if you have been at fault and not produced him to do well. The horse won't know. All he will understand is that if he touches a pole, his rider will be grumpy! So hopefully he will try harder to shut his rider up! It goes without saying that you should be cooing 'Good boy' when he does try hard and makes every effort to jump cleanly.

Pat 'n' push is the ideal exercise to take the opportunity to criticise. It's short and snappy and when a rattle occurs be short and snappy with your grumbling too. It's no good grumbling when the horse is three strides on after the jump, that's much too late.

If the rider grumbles in the middle of a longer exercise with more jumping elements, it can make things worse if the horse panics and rushes through the rest of the sequence, hitting even more poles. Pat 'n' push is, therefore, uniquely suitable for this sort of remedial treatment, ensuring the horse gets it right before tackling a longer sequence.

The helper's contribution to the success of the exercise

Helpers, your input to this particular exercise is vital because you can get close to the action and concentrate on observing the position of the horse's hind legs or feet as he takes off at the second jump. It sounds pretty simple, and it is.

Study the diagram and photos so that you are quite clear about what the horse should be doing with his feet at the first jump and in the middle of the distance. Pat 'n' push is a great exercise for your rider to take away from a training session and one that many trainers would recommend as 'homework' between lessons. If you have attended the training session, you will have seen what's happening too, and you'll soon have the confidence to give advice when you and your rider are working alone, especially when that proffered advice works.

You'll soon get the hang of concentrating on what the horse is doing with his hind feet in the middle of the distance, and will be able pass this on to your rider. (Figures 15.2a–c and 15.3a–d)

When the horse is pinging through the bounce, not too high to start with and with both crosses the same height, you will soon be able to get your eye in and tell, and show, your rider how far apart the horse's feet are when they push off the ground for the second cross.

The closer together the feet are, the more power the rider is producing, the better and steeper the jumping effort generated. If the positioning of the feet is fairly wide, the horse will only be cantering over the jumps rather than putting the effort in to get over them higher and more cleanly. Unless some more energy is gathered up on the approach and in the

Figures 15.2a–c a) Wes charging in to the pat 'n' push in a hurry with legs everywhere as he takes the first jump (**b**) and things are no better going out over the second element (**c**). Not the neat and tidy exercise Phoebe hoped for.

Figures 15.3a–d a) Phoebe has Wes approaching in a steadier canter, and he is better going in landing smack dab in the middle of the distance (**b**) and doing a great job going out: not quite the perfect 'push', but pretty close (**c**); and (**d**) Alison's happy too!

95

middle of the distance the horse will start to rattle the poles when they get higher.

The wide-stance canter position in the middle will not give enough power and energy to get strongly and more vertically off the ground. It indicates a bit of a casual take-off, not much more effort than a normal canter stride, which will just not give enough oomph to jump really well, especially when the jumps become more demanding.

The sharper shorter position or placing of the feet will enable the horse to push up a bit more as he takes off.

Hopefully the horse's canter approach will allow him to 'pat' the floor lightly with both front feet as he lands in the middle, and 'push' strongly behind as he jumps out (Figures 15.4a–c).

This work needs to be encouraged for *every* jumping effort, and repeated and repeated until it

becomes more or less automatic and routine. Ten, twenty times, even more, keep them going until they hit fewer poles; there is no time limit on this exercise.

It is quite straightforward to spot if the horse is wide or close with his feet in the middle of the distance and you can feel pretty confident with the reporting of what you see. And the more the rider gets the 'feel' of how to produce that 'push' in the middle they can start trying to get that same 'up' feeling at the first cross too.

When they are going well and ready to raise the second jump, lower the first cross, you don't want to build something which would be impossible for them to jump well, and the bigger the 'out' jump, the smaller the 'in' jump should be. Don't let the rider relax the way she rides in.

All of the jumps need to be ridden accurately, so working just as hard over a reduced cross will

Figures 15.4a–c a) At the beginning of the session Nicky is a touch too forward too soon and Domino is literally just cantering over the jump; there is no spring. What a difference after a few efforts: this 'push' is lovely (**b**). He now maintains exactly the same stylish and strong 'push' whatever he's jumping and is going up not just along (**c**).

stand them in good stead for jumping round a course when there are no crosses at all. The back feet need to be produced well under him and 'pushing' just the same.

You must keep helping them by maintaining a running commentary on the hind leg position, especially when the horse starts to improve, as he surely will if the rider recognises and acts on these guidelines.

And if the hind leg is strong and pushy and the horse is kicking poles out, the same pat 'n' push practice will give your rider the chance to sort out and prevent any avoidable knockdowns.

This is a very different sort of exercise to the course practice sessions as everything will happen far more quickly in this single exercise. Up until now it has been fairly easy for both of you to be in accord in recognising the mistakes made in cutting corners or riding the better lines to get the better canter. Now your rider will need a split-second observation from you and you will have to be sharp and decisive. Even experienced riders find it difficult occasionally to feel which leg or hoof has kicked out a pole. If your rider doesn't know, you should be able to spot the culprits and hopefully not be timid about saying what you see even if you aren't sure why. Then you will be able to suggest trying the various remedies to prevent the rattles. One of them will work.

It may not be easy for the rider to effect that remedy, but with your eagle eye on her case it won't be hard to understand and she will know what she's striving for.

If she accepts that you aren't trying to train her, merely observe rather than tell her what to do, then a valuable session is possible.

Front-leg rattles

Causes

If the horse rattles poles with his front legs, usually the causes are pretty simple and the rider has a choice of methods to try to prevent this happening.

If the horse has patted the ground nicely between the jumps and pushed with the hind feet close together and still knocks the 'out' fence down, the prime reason is the rider's timing.

When the canter is successful, strong, powerful and consistent it will be much easier for a rider to anticipate the take-off point and go into the jumping position prematurely. So what happens then? They suffer for going well!

There are two consequences:

1. The rider pushes her hands forward as the horse is about to take off, resulting in an immediate loss of impulsion as all the energy gathered is released too early allowing the horse to travel along rather than up.

2. The rider swings her weight too forward over his shoulder as he is about to come up off the ground resulting in more weight over his shoulder and front legs and so he doesn't snap them up so cleanly.

Any rider will be quite capable of committing both sins at the same time in one exercise.

Remedies

The following is the advice that you can offer, fairly sure that one or all of the comments will hit the spot.

If the rider tries one remedy and it doesn't work, move on to the next. Whatever you're suggesting won't be wrong, just maybe not the exact one to fit the situation. It is a very simple exercise to execute, but not easy to get it right every time.

Although you might not be too sure of the reasons, and sometimes it needs a much practised eye to spot exactly what is happening in the middle of the crosses, any or all of the advice offered will still hold good; just parrot away with the following comments to remind the rider what they should be striving for.

• Use more leg, but no faster.

• Make a very conscious effort to exaggerate looking up. It's fairly difficult to be too forward if you are looking up enough.

• Wait for the horse's neck or crest to come up to meet your chest rather than bobbing down into the jumping position too early.

- Try to let your hinges – your hips, knees and ankles – be soft and allow your weight to hang off the stirrup bars, not bump about on the back of the saddle.

- Don't shoot your hands forward in the mistaken belief that it will 'free his head'. A sloppy or erratic contact will result in a sloppy and erratic jump.

If they are still kicking poles out in front, ask your rider to try a little tweak, or check, with her contact, a quick half-halt if you prefer, just as they are about to come off the ground in the middle of the bounce. Don't let her think she is being asked to haul the horse's front legs off the ground. The aim of trying this is to draw the horse's hind legs underneath him a little further so he can get a more vertical take-off.

The rider's leg needs to be nudging at the same time so that the coordination works. It's no good trying a tweak if she hasn't got impulsion too, she doesn't need the horse thinking she wants him to stop!

If her timing is right, it should be very effective. If it doesn't work to start with, keep trying.

Hind-leg rattles

Study Diagram 8; If the rider does not collect the horse as he jumps in to the bounce he will be casual with his hind legs and the impulsion being produced will clearly not be enough. And the impulsion that must be produced needs to be gathered up in a split second. If the hind legs are wide apart and unable to generate enough 'up' energy to stay precise the timing from the rider is not good enough. She has not used enough leg in the middle to produce enough energy to encourage him to work harder off the ground and snap his hind legs up sharply and neatly.

The horse may well jump cleanly when the crosses are small, but once the exercise progresses and the height of the crosses or second jump is increased, there is no chance of lolloping along in a less than powerful canter and staying accurate.

So, if poles roll, what has the rider done wrong? Perhaps it isn't immediately obvious to you but that needn't prevent you offering some of your stock phrases to the rider, which will eventually prove to be the right cure.

A likely cause is: 'too forward too soon' and you have to try to spot if the rider has swung her weight too forward too soon, bobbing down to meet the horse's neck instead of timing it right and allowing his head and neck to come up to meet her chest. If the hands have pushed forward on landing after the first cross and given away the contact vital for the energetic push in the middle as the horse is coming up off the ground at the second cross, it allows the horse to be casual and careless as he takes off. The strong pushy hind legs have simply not been produced and he hasn't been gathered enough to make the exercise easy for him to perform successfully.

Too forward too soon doesn't just cause front-leg knock-downs; if your rider hasn't put enough leg on in the middle or hasn't timed the leg aids to be productive, he will still kick poles out behind. The horse always needs to be pushed from the leg at the point of take-off and if this aid hasn't been applied with the right timing, the horse isn't being helped and encouraged to get 'up' from a powerful hind-leg approach.

As helper you can be perfectly secure in the knowledge that if you offer any or all of the following advice, any or all of the suggestions will be valid.

Run through the suggestions used to help the front-leg hitches as the rider must be reminded how to gather up all the energy with the balance and contact, and try to stay in a stable and secure position throughout the exercise.

Remedies

- The rider must look up and be careful not to be too forward or give the contact away at the take-off point.

- The horse's front end must be supported as always.

- The rider must make the **extra effort** using more leg, a good healthy nudge, in a coordinated effort to push and hold him into a more condensed outline in the middle of the crosses, the basic remedy for better back legs.

- Remember, the suggestion 'More leg, but no faster' just about covers every eventuality!

- If more power is being generated and the contact is supporting him consistently, he can't escape working harder.

- The only way for him to go is up and the back feet will be in the ideal position to pat 'n' push. And the horse *will* go up; he will pat 'n' push sharper and more cleanly, especially if the rider recognises the nice springy feel and tries to produce it at the 'in' jump too.

There is another tip that should be considered to prevent disappointment: encourage your rider to stay up in her jumping position a little longer when actually in the air over the jump. When the jump is springy and the horse is trying hard, it would be easy for her to anticipate landing and come down a little too soon in the saddle. If she changes her weight to land while the horse is still over the jump, he will also prepare to land sooner and put his undercarriage down early, resulting in a rub behind. Just tell her to hover in position a split second longer; you will both be surprised at the improvement it will make to his accuracy if she keeps off his back until he is well clear of the poles. After all, what will happen if she hovers longer than necessary? Nothing awful; just cleaner jumping.

Summary

It is difficult to say what is causing a careless or casual mode of jumping with 100 per cent accuracy, especially if the helper is not an expert, *but* the rider is on pretty safe ground if she recognises or assumes that nine times out of ten front-leg rattles can be eliminated by a better, supportive and more consistent contact. Equally, hind-leg rattles are generally caused by not enough leg to produce the impulsion required. And it's fairly uncomplicated to work it out.

- If the rider tries to hold more throughout the exercise, she will soon recognise if there is an improvement in front.

- Likewise if she uses more leg and hold, the hind-leg rattles should also vanish.

- A rider might find working this way with a helper to be more trial and error than working with an experienced trainer, but once you and your rider have settled on the plan of action which is working, don't forget it. Most problems tend to creep back in and will be repeated as the rider starts to relax when things are going well. Remember the bicycle analogy: if you stop pedaling consistently, the bicycle stops going forward so smoothly and consistently!

- Quick fixes won't work. The only successful long-term solution is to ride better and make sure the horse understands that the rider is cross if he touches a pole. If the horse is well ridden and understands that the poles are not to be touched, he will try harder too.

EXERCISE 9

The tripod or clover leaf

PURPOSE OF THE EXERCISE

This exercise can be used either in combination with the whole course or can be practised alone as a major challenge. With the addition of two more crosses or jumps at X and Y together with cross A, you have all the kit necessary to improve the four major aims of the Foolproof work.

1. The quality of the canter; to keep going round the turns without stuttering.

2. Steering and accurate route judgment, looking far enough ahead while still producing the impulsion.

3. Flying changes and dealing with the disunited canter when it happens.

4. Jump-off turns, pace and angles.

Check Diagrams 9a and 9b, see opposite. **Easier option – 9a**: you will work on the **right rein** to blue cross A, to cross X, to cross Y, to cross X, to cross Y, repeating the turns over X and Y. **More difficult option – 9b**: you will work on the **right rein**, to cross X, to cross Y, to cross X, to cross Y, repeating the turns over X and Y, and finishing the exercise over blue cross A.

Green route = good route

Red route = bad route

Setting up the exercise

As with most of the work involving the grid fences or crosses, the tripod exercise can be ridden two ways, the simple route or the far more challenging second option.

- If you are setting up the tripod to use on its own and are working in a field, try to position the tripod against the fence. You can do with a boundary to stop you going too wide and losing the value of the work.

- Give yourself markers or poles to restrict the width of the exercise, 30m (98ft) will be a sensible option.

- Make sure your helper knows where you plan to go, so they can keep out of the way, the jumps come up very quickly as you ought to plan to keep going over at least eight or ten jumping efforts.

- With this exercise you also need to show your helper how to count strides; the number of strides you take round the loops will become very significant when you are practising jump-off turns.
  - If you do fewer strides on a turn, you should do a quicker time without rushing and risking knock-downs.
  - Also, the loops that you ride will be far more consistent if you can produce the same number of strides from jump to jump and it's something you should definitely be aiming for. By counting the number of strides it will be easy for you and your helper to recognise if you are managing your turns equally or not.

Diagram 9a

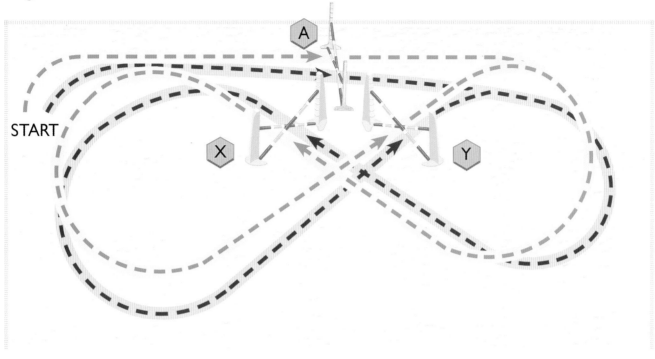

Diagram 9b

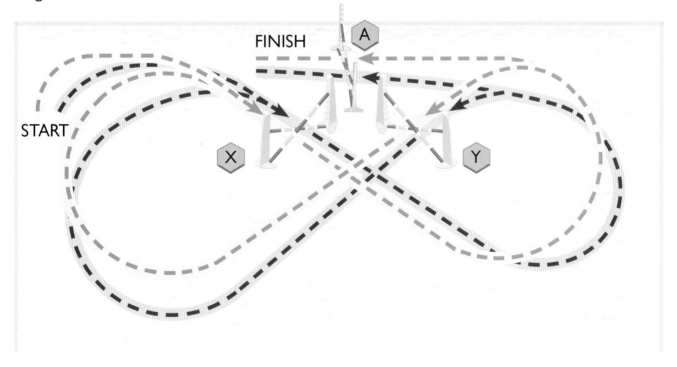

- Do not distract yourself from the riding; get your helper to count for you.
- Make sure your helper doesn't start counting the strides until after the horse has landed. It will be a learning curve for them to get used to ignoring the take-off and landing, it's the actual number of true non-jumping strides on the ground that you want to tot up.

• Your helper will be able to give you valuable input to each and every aspect of these tripod exercises.

The easier route

The canter

The jumps remain in the same place for both options of the exercise, so plan to tackle the easier route first (Diagram 9a). The quality of the canter can be practised every inch of the way.

- Start on the right rein at A and then make a three-quarter turn to X, then ride from X to Y, and then Y to X.
- Repeat the turns over X and Y.

If you stop riding consistently or lean in round the crosses your helper will notice more quickly than you that the horse is not working with his hind leg sufficiently underneath himself to maintain the canter rhythm. Your helper will see his hind leg start to stutter slightly before you feel it.

Remedy

Keep your inside shoulder up, use more outside rein and inside leg and steer a little wider for the extremity of the turn so that it isn't quite so hard for the horse to keep working in a strong rhythm. The more you repeat the work, the more likely your horse will be to cut in as he will be quite certain where he's going, and so this is all good practice for you to keep him out and the canter strong.

Steering

If you struggle with your steering, the relentless attention to turning accurately needed to negotiate and complete this exercise will tell you instantly what you are doing wrong. If you listen to what your helper is telling you, you will be well on the way to improving the navigation. It will be so easy for the helper to spot the slightest deviation from the ideal track to be ridden.

Remedy

Use wiggle poles; it's far better to help the horse initially to take the better line. If the horse is cutting in, your helper can place the wiggle pole on the inside of the hoped-for track to encourage you to keep the horse out.

If your reactions to turning are a bit slow, a wiggle pole on the outside extremity of your turn will help you guide the horse round without bulging.

You may think you are looking far enough ahead, but your helper will be able to see exactly when you turn your head to actually look round the turn, and mostly it will be too late. If they say this is what you're doing, listen to them. You can exaggerate turning your head to look where you hope to be going, earlier rather than later, so that the horse can pick up on your body language. Your helper will also be able to nag you if you begin to drop your inside shoulder, something that is so plain for an observer to see, but hard for you to recognise how susceptible you may be to that particular error (Figures 16.1a–e, opposite, and 16.2a–d, see overleaf).

The more difficult route

Study the more difficult route (Diagram 9b).

- Start on the right rein and approach cross X from a square corner into the right turn (Figures 16.3a and b, see overleaf).
- A stride away from cross X, make a positive effort to take a stronger contact with your right rein to hold him out for after the jump.
- Keep your left shoulder up. It is almost irresistible to lean into the fresh turn and drop your weight and your shoulder down as you jump. And if you do so, you will probably land on the wrong leg. Exaggerate

Figure 16.1a–e a–d) Alena and Claude tackle the Tripod Y jump having made a great pat 'n' push. The wiggle pole helps Alena to encourage Claude to stay straight and keep out into his new outside rein. Alena holds well over the jump but drops her shoulder slightly on landing and is a little giving with the contact. **e)** Now the wiggle pole looks unnecessary, they are following a great line and Alena's shoulders are level, she is well in charge of the steering.

Above **Figure 16.2a–d**
Christopher is a very different horse to the neat and nimble Claude; he has a big stride and Becca's helper has been nagging her to be tough with the new outside rein for the turn after cross Y. It has obviously worked as she is quick to gather him up on landing and gets a top-class right canter within a couple of strides.

Right **Figures 16.3a and b**
Hannah has ridden Willow into an impeccable corner on the arena and the resulting approach and jump at cross X is just about perfect.

keeping your new inside shoulder up, weight into the outside stirrup, and it should be fine.

- If he still lands on the wrong leg or disunited, ignore it and carry on round the loop to cross Y (Figures 16.4a–c, below and 16.5a–d, see overleaf).

Flying changes; cantering disunited; wrong lead

This exercise is a foolproof method for allowing your horse to develop true flying changes. All the riders I see prefer a true lead round a course of jumps, in fact they become positively stressed if they are disunited or on the wrong leg and fuss about it instead of doing the sensible thing, as described in the remedy below.

Your helper will be able to see if you are wrong so if you generally look down to see if you are on the correct lead, *don't do it*. Stay level and rely on your helper to chant 'wrong leg' or 'disunited'. They will soon get the hang of spotting it and let you know immediately if the canter is not what you hope for.

Remedy
Firstly, don't get worked up about it; keep going, even if it feels uncomfortable and you don't like it. Your horse will not learn to sort his legs out if you keep protectively bringing him back to trot and trying again.

It is fairly unusual for your horse to be disunited in front, although certainly not unheard of. In this case, resist the temptation to lean in to try to get him to change, just keep pushing him into your outside

Figures 16.4a–c Bex and Muddle take the more difficult route (Diagram 9b) out on the grass with only a marker pole to help the turn instead of a fence. Muddle jumps nicely in the middle to get a good canter away to begin the left turn round to jump Y.

Figure 16.5a–d The more difficult route (Diagram 9b) On the approach to Y the canter stays consistently strong and Muddle jumps it very neatly from the more tricky short approach.

Notice how quickly Bex then takes charge of the canter and the turn round to X by having a very supporting new outside rein. Because Bex is so level, Muddle's canter lead is faultless.

hand, maintaining a supporting contact and give him every opportunity to change without being harassed. He will be finding it just as uncomfortable round these demanding turns as you do and will be pleased to return to a more balanced canter himself.

Far more common is correct lead in front and disunited behind. This will often occur because, again, you have leaned in to get correct canter instead of staying level and you haven't turned his head slightly to the outside as you ask.

Keep your weight more into the outside stirrup so that you lighten the load on the inside hind leg. He will then find it easier to bring the inside leg through and correct his balance and take true canter.

If he is finding the tripod exercise very difficult, make the loops larger to give him more room to actually stay in canter. Usually by the time he has jumped another cross he will be righting himself as long as you don't try to lean in to your new turn.

The more you stay calm and repeat the exercise, the more often he will land and canter away in true lead. Once you've both got the hang of the exercise and you are consistently not allowing him to cut in to the turn after the cross, you should find that he starts to do a flying change initially over the cross, and then progress to changing legs a stride before he takes off as he recognises where he is going.

The helper's contribution to the success of the exercise

Listen to your helper's observations; they will be invaluable for this exercise as they can really help with the 'prevention is better than cure' principles. Your helper should keep up a commentary to remind you to keep riding consistently.

- If you are trying to improve your canter, then don't drop down to trot. Your helper must be positively scathing if you become too protective and trot to change.

- Your helper should pounce on you with 'more leg', 'go wider' and 'look where you're going'. Any or all three of these comments will be helpful even if you think you are perfect and will remind you to keep up the hard work, so take notice of them and don't argue.

- The helper needs eyes like a hawk to discern any hint of tipping in over the crosses and when they spot it, they must let you know in no uncertain terms. It will be easier for them to spot you tipping than for you to recognise this little failing for yourself!

(Figures 16.6a and b)

As with all the other exercises, repetition will be the key to success, but give yourself some breathing space.

Try to do eight or ten jumping efforts and then have a break. Frequently the horse will come back to the exercise and start again better than he left off. It takes time for them to recognise how much easier it is to canter round the loops on true lead especially if you keep wriggling about trying to sort out the lead for him!

Don't try cutting in and making the turns more acute in the hope that it will force him to take the correct leg.

Be persistent and calm and allow him to work it out. If you are giving him the correct signals and not trying to lean into the lead, he will get the hang of it.

Summary

The tripod exercise is also such a good work-out to practise over and over. When you are managing both routes comfortably you can see that it would be fairly simple to amalgamate both exercises by starting off with the easier work for three or four turns and then going wide and taking in the other route to jump the more difficult approaches. Mix and match the routes to keep the horse listening and responsive to your steering.

Figures 16.6a and b a) It is always a good idea for your helper to get behind, or (**b**) bravely head on, for a different view.

16.7 Great landing from left to right rein: well-balanced, new true lead from Louie.

Whichever way you ride it, the relentless consistency needed to do well will help you to develop all the skills to help you do better in jump-off situations. The planned routes are ideal for practising your steering, turns and jump ability as the horse is presented with a choice of two jumps as he comes off the turn. You and your helper will know if you've done a good job when your horse doesn't try to cart you to the wrong option.

Counting the number of strides between jumps will provide concrete evidence to let you know if you are reducing the number of strides taken and the distance travelled.

Try to navigate shorter routes rather than go faster, and if your horse has a marked preference to do a sharper turn on one rein, remember and use it to your advantage at a competition. And conversely, if he's not quite so good on the other rein, practise it more at home but be prepared to go a little wider when you're out competing.

Jumping on the angle will also give you quicker turns; think how easy it has been for your horse to cut in while you try to prevent it! Occasionally you can allow it and call it jump-off practice.

Just like all the other suggested exercises, you will get out of it as much as you put in, but you and your helper can rest assured that the improvement in your jumping is there for the taking.

EXERCISE 10

The tramline figure of eight

PURPOSE OF THE EXERCISE

This exercise, like the others, is aimed at producing and consolidating the strong, active Foolproof canter so that your horse adjusts to arrive at a jump with enough impulsion to get over it easily and accurately, hopefully from the take-off point that you find comfortable. You still want to think of the corners coming into the jumps as being a little square, and the exercise should be ridden as a figure of eight, changing rein each time you go through the tramlines.

This exercise will help all horses as demonstrated by the variety of types in the following photos: a young small horse, a novice tall horse, an arrogant and bossy horse, a silly 'bulging' horse, a lazy 'slanting' horse and two hefty middleweights. They will all inevitably improve their ability or attitude as the sheer continuity of the work enables the rider to practise all the canter and steering skills required for improvement.

As with the other figure-of-eight exercises, although not the main aim, if it is well ridden the tramline exercise will give the horses every opportunity to be allowed to learn to execute true flying changes.

Check Diagrams 10a, 10b, 10c and 10d overleaf. **Diagrams 10a** and **10b** show the placing of the tramlines and jumps X and Y and the tramline route on the marked-out grass arena. They show the faults in the turns (10a: slanted turn; 10b: overshot turn) and the correct routes. Starting on the **left rein** you will ride **through the tramlines** and make a **right turn to take jump Y**, then continue on the **right rein all the way round through 360 degrees to go straight through the tramlines again,** then make a **left turn to take jump X** and continue **round 360 degrees to the tramlines once more** to complete, then repeat, the figure-of-eight sequence.

Diagrams 10c and 10d show the tramline exercise on the course arena. The additional jumps make the exercise a demanding one to do well.

Green route = good route

Red route = bad route

Setting up the exercise

The tramline exercise is very plain and straightforward to set up, using two jumps and a pair of wiggle poles, the tramlines, either on the arena or in the field.

- The placing of the jumps is as compact as you want it to be and your helper will be able to keep their eye on you all the way round the 360 degree turn. It will be obvious to them if you get sloppy when you are not actually facing a jump.

- The main difficulty with this exercise is steering the sensible track and having enough confidence to push straight through the tramline wiggle poles and not turn to the jump too early or too late.

- It really doesn't matter how far apart the two jumps are as long as the tramlines are set to be in the middle of the distance between them. The closer they are the better for the success of the exercise, 20m (66ft) would be fine, but it's not essential. Place them a bit wider apart to start with if you wish as long as the tramlines are still guiding you to the middle of the distance.
  - Your helper can alter them easily as you become more practised.

Diagram 10a

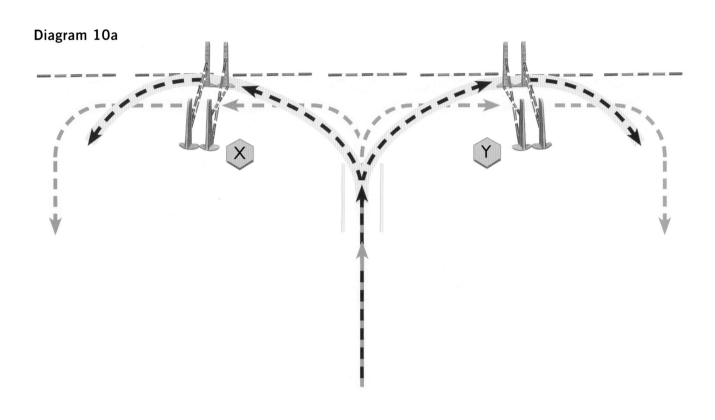

Diagram 10b

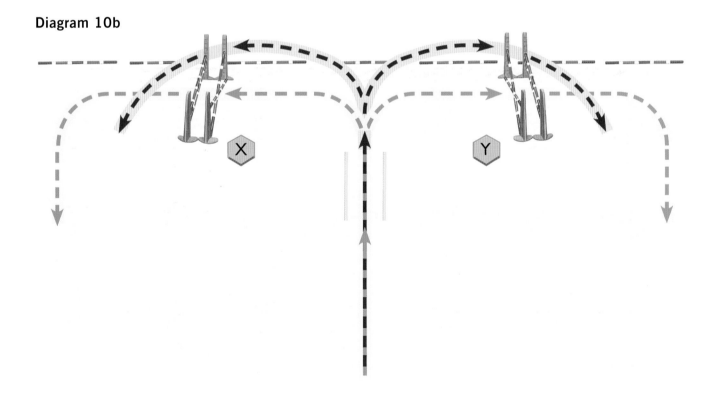

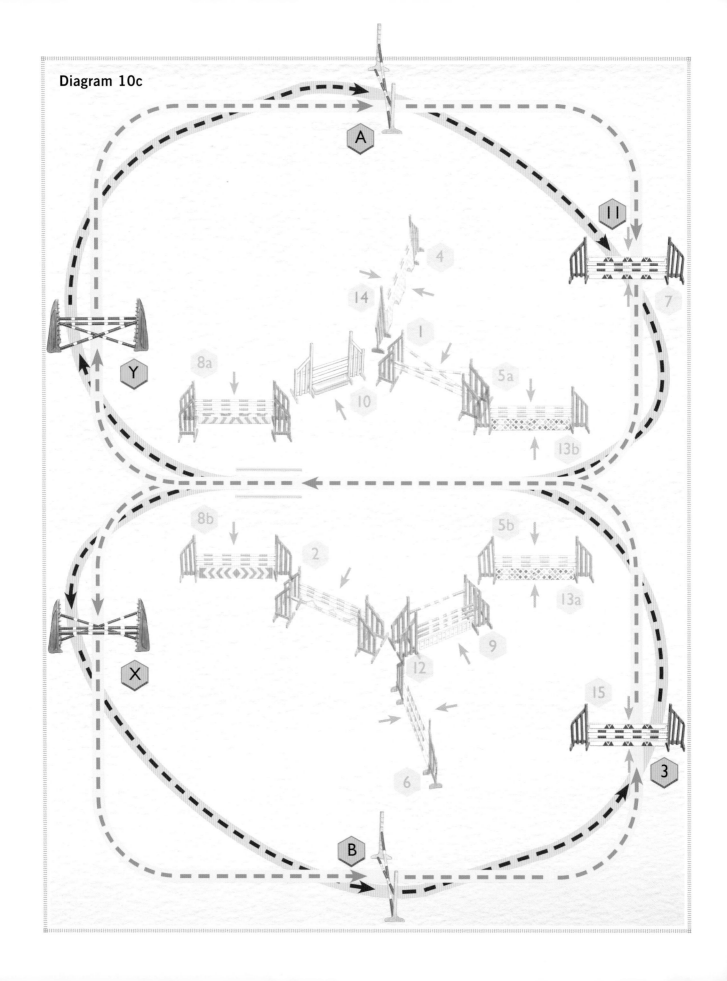

Diagram 10c

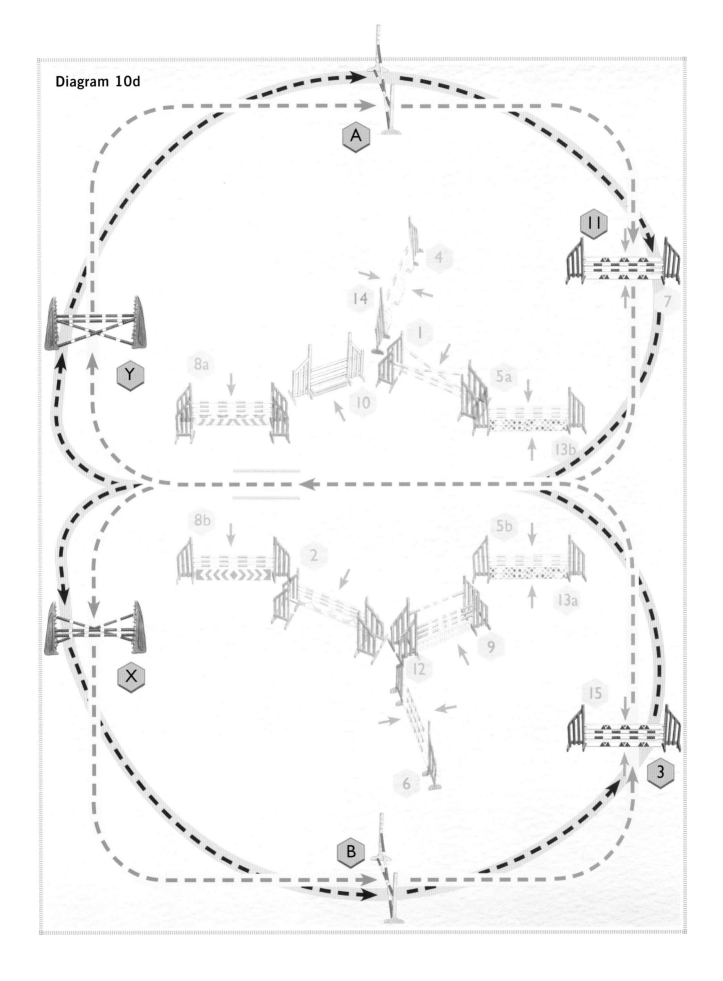

Diagram 10d

- You are hoping to have a similar turn and jump in each direction so you do need the guide poles to be symmetrically positioned.

- The jumps need to be a comfortable size to start with, you want to be concentrating on your route and canter quality rather than the size of the jump.

  - It will be very easy for your helper to increase the size of the jumps as your stride pattern becomes more consistent.

The successful tramline exercise encourages true flying changes

The youngsters

The first two horses of the horses demonstrating this exercise are Maybe and Louie. Maybe is a 15.2hh, chunky middleweight youngster and this is a fairly demanding exercise to ask of her, but Isobel is supporting her well. Louie too is a young horse but is a very different shape and size to Maybe; he is tall and lanky. Lizzy is concentrating on guiding him accurately and square-on through the tramlines, and producing flying changes instead of disunited turns is a very welcome bonus to the exercise. (Figures 17.1a–e and 17.2a–g)

Figures 17.1a–e a) Isobel has entered the tramlines from the left rein and in left canter. **b)** Maybe is asked to turn right and Isobel has made every effort to steer right while keeping her new outside rein (left rein) supportive and her weight level. **c)** Maybe gives a great response as she does a neat flying change, because she has been given the opportunity to do so. Well done Isobel for making it a possibility. **d)** A nice strong exit from the tramlines resulting in (**e**) a lovely effort over jump Y.

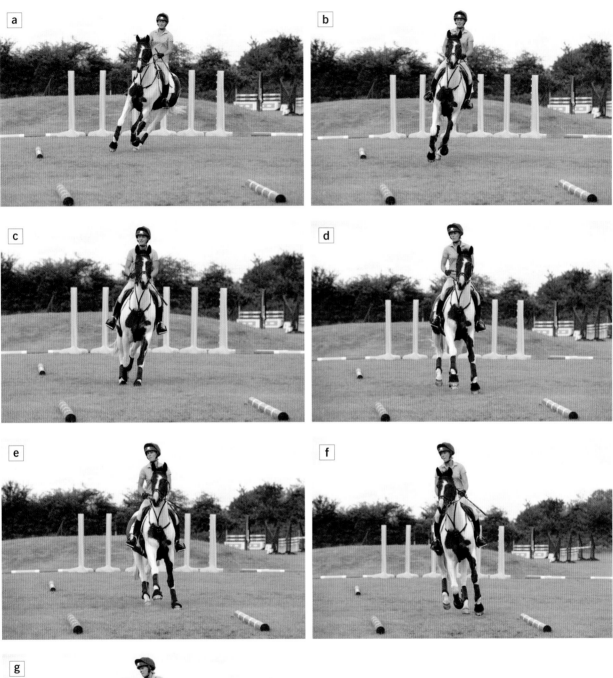

Figures 17.2a–g When standing head-on to your rider you can see that the tramline work has added benefits as well as improving the steering: Lizzy produced a really nice left canter, squared up well to the tramlines and kept her weight level enabling Louie to execute a perfect flying change to right canter and a great exit right to Y. Note the wiggle pole to help Lizzy steer more accurately off her turn to the tramlines.

RIDING THE EXERCISE

- Start off on the left rein and ride a nice turn to the poles without cutting in so that you are pretty straight when you get there.

- Try very hard to keep your shoulders level as you go through the tramlines and before you get to the end of the poles you should have a nice supportive feel with your **new outside rein**, **the left rein**, to prevent you cutting in to jump Y.

- The turn from your right-hand steering should be positive and persistent. Don't start the turn and fail to complete the steering, otherwise your horse will jump off centre and towards the boundary.

- If you ride the sort of turn you've been working so hard to achieve your horse should find the short approach positively beneficial and the jump easy.

- Carry on round on the right rein and try to ride an accurate line round the 360 degrees to get straight again to the tramlines and then prepare to turn left to jump X. by supporting the **new outside rein**, **the right rein**, before you actually turn. Don't give the new outside rein away to help you turn, do more with your new inside steering hand.

Remember that preparation is the key to giving your horse the best shot to the jumps, so holding a bit more with the *new* outside rein while you are still going straight though the tramlines will get you round the corner with plenty of energy; as long as you also remember to steer with the inside hand.

Tramline problems

The arrogant and bossy horse

If you are finding it difficult preventing your horse from taking charge and anticipating the turns, you will be losing some of the benefit of the tramline exercise, so try another approach, literally, as Emma had to with Katie! (Figures 17.3a–d and 17.4a and b)

If you head for the tramlines from the left rein, instead of turning right handed, keep steering left to cross X and stay on the left rein for two or three more jumps. Make sure it is *you* calling the shots and vary the exercise according to the level of anticipation and cooperation from your horse.

You don't have to ride the figure of eight uncompromisingly, just stay in charge and decide which way you need to turn to establish the good turns and canter; think on the hoof! And make sure you think ahead of your clever horse so you can contain his enthusiasm.

Slanting and overshooting on the turns

Check Diagrams 10a and 10b.

As you can see from Diagram 10a, if you turn too early and slant the turn, your line to the fence will be slanted too. You don't have a good chance for your horse to pat 'n' push the ground on take-off. It will be a bit hit and miss as he won't have the power to adjust his stride to cope easily. And if you misjudge the exit and overshoot, i.e. bulge out, through the poles before you turn, Diagram 10b, you will find it difficult to straighten up for a square approach to the jumps.

The lazy 'slanting' horse

Frex is a big horse who can't see the point in working *too* hard. He is pretty versatile and leans in equally well on both reins and when he wants to cut a corner it's hard to keep him out. The tramline exercise is ideal to help Jo keep him gathered up and working. (Figures 17.5a–c, 17.6a–e and 17.7a and b, see overleaf)

The silly 'bulging' horse

Spider is careless and leaps before he looks; he has a tendency to overshoot a turn or bulge out (Figures 17.8a–c, 17.9 a–e and 17.10a–d, see overleaf).

Carry on round the exercise and try to do at least six or eight jumping efforts in one go. If you are doing good turns on every corner and are nice and straight as you approach the tramlines, your horse will have every chance to start throwing in some flying changes, another great benefit with this exercise.

Above **Figures 17.3a–d** Naughty Katie has decided she knows where she's going and is totally ignoring Emma's suggestion to cooperate en route to Y. Not very comfortable!

Below **Figures 17.4a and b** Emma's mother Fiona could be forgiven for being a little exasperated with Katie's wilfulness and makes the common-sense suggestion that Emma tries to conceal her intentions and take Katie by surprise by jumping X from the left rein instead of staying rigidly on the figure of eight.
Wise move; well done Mum!

Figures 17.5a–c a and b) Frex is quite happy to cut in on both reins to X and Y. Although Jo is doing her best to keep him out, he uses his weight against her. **c)** An uncomfortable jump; Jo needs to take a stronger *new* outside rein sooner through the tramlines to hold him out on the turn, and then steer with the inside hand to X.

As with the Tripod work, your shoulders must be level on the turns, try hard not to lean in and keep encouraging with your leg the whole time. It is a very backward step to check to give yourself time to look where you're going and keep nudging away, don't allow your horse to drop into trot.

You should be judging your route so that it is wide enough for you to stay in the strong canter but not so wide that you are bulging out on your corners.

The helper's contribution to the success of the exercise

As always you, the helper, will be a huge asset in helping your rider to get the most benefit from this exercise, primarily because you will be able to see what is going on, especially as the exercise will be more effective as it is repeated and you will start to get your eye in. It will soon be very apparent if they are getting to X and Y with no power and poor shots, so don't be shy about telling them. You should know the drill by the time your rider tries this exercise.

The middleweights

Look at the next two subjects, two middleweight horses, Bob and Diego, and two lightweight riders, Sian and Evie. However fit and strong the girls are they must be encouraged to think ahead of their horses and recognise that they must seize the initiative before things go pear shaped and the horses physically get the better of them! (Figures 17.11a–d, 17.12, 17.13a–d, 17.14, 17.15a–d and 17.16a–c)

Above and left
Figures 17.6a–e a–c) More positive through the tramlines; much better canter and straighter to X. **d–e)** Still very slightly on the slant but a much better approach and jump at X.

Far left and left
Figures 17.7a and b Good turn equals straight Frex and level Jo.

Figures 17.10a–d a) Progress! Spider is starting to accept Mary's guidance round the tramline exercise, but is it enough to make him listen to her? **b–d)** Mary takes him away from the tramlines to put him to the test; here he's concentrating and steadier off the bank: a great canter and an easy jump.

Opposite page, top row **Figures 17.8a–c a)** Spider before practising the Foolproof exercises is hopeless as he leaps before he looks. Mary tries to steady Spider off the little drop so he has time to spot the skinny, but he turns a deaf ear. **b and c)** The inevitable result as his legs have gone faster than his brain.

Opposite page, centre and bottom row **Figures 17.9a–d** Here Spider has argued with Mary round the tramline exercise, *overshot* the turn to Y expecting to go past the jump and simply not seen the jump until the last second but she doesn't give in and let him go his own way. His amazing scope and ability helps him explode over the fence, but it's not ideal or comfortable for Mary. When the exercise is repeated Mary chooses the jumps at random; sometimes going the same way three times in a row. By not sticking to the figure-of-eight route he doesn't know where he's going unless he listens to what Mary is telling him to do.

Figures 17.11a–d a) Sian has tried hard to prevent Bob cutting in too early through the tramlines to jump X and although the canter is strong he is determined to slant to the jump and loses some hind leg impulsion on the way. She must be more suspicious and be ready sooner to prevent him even starting to cut in instead of hoping it won't happen. **b–d)** He takes off without enough push, jumps across the fence with inevitable results and is still heading to the right as he lands. **Helper's comments** Recite your mantra: 'More leg but no faster, shoulder up, don't cut in, don't tip, turn your head, keep hold, push and wait'.

Figure 17.12 Quick Beryl, your daughter is waiting to come the other way!

Top row and above **Figures 17.13a–d a)** Sian is quicker to support with her *new* outside rein through the tramlines; great flying change! **b and c)** A squarer turn to the middle of X and (**d**) a much better jumping effort.

Right **Figure 17.14** All that hard work, practise and nagging from Beryl to insist Bob jumps in the middle pays off.

Above **Figures 17.15a–d** Evie and Diego are doing exactly the same wrong things. Evie produces a nice canter from the right rein but allows Diego to slant in to jump X after the turn. The cross poles help to straighten him up but the approach is not easy and he has to try very hard to jump cleanly. **Helper's comments** Evie's helper should, like Sian's, be reciting the mantra: 'More leg, shoulder up, don't cut in, don't tip, turn your head, keep hold, push and wait'.

Below **Figures 17.16a–c a and b)** Another slanting turn and with the more difficult planks he can't stay clean. Evie's weight is unlevel to her right and it is Diego's right foreleg that kicks the plank off. **c)** A straighter approach, Evie's weight is level, and Diego is spot on. With Diego's tendency to cut corners apparent in the tramline exercises, Evie's helper could have anticipated what they would do at the planks. Diego is much better at the second attempt from a squarer turn. **Helpers comments** 'More outside rein on the turn, keep the shoulders level and don't go too forward to the jump. Better, but you're still too forward even when he jumps cleanly.'

If the horse makes a bad job of the work to start with, run through the suggestions until one of them works and the horse jumps better.

- Remember what your rider has a tendency to get wrong. It would be no surprise to see that she would be a repeater, and will lapse again into the same bad habit unless you stay on her case and keep reminding her.

- You need to be mobile so you can nip about from side to side to keep an eye on any tendency to cut corners or lean in on the approaches to X and Y.

- A head-on view to the tramlines will be perfect to check the straightness of the approaches but if there is no fence between you and the jumps do be careful.

- Don't trust your rider 100 per cent to turn in time. They certainly wouldn't mow you down deliberately, but a few times I've had to nip out of the way quickly when my riders are concentrating on what they are doing and forget to look far enough ahead. You don't want to be trampled in the process; poor payment for being an asset!

- Do be careful where you stand. If your rider gets it wrong, they may well blame you for being in the wrong place and distracting the horse.

- The rear is also a good place to watch from, it will be so very easy to see exactly what your rider is doing through the tramlines in terms of shoulder up and accurate steering on the turns.
  - Stand to one side of the approach and then as they go past you step in to place yourself right behind them so that your vision is crystal clear. It is so much easier to spot the faults if you are on the route they have taken. And you won't be as alarmed as observing from the head on view when you wonder if they are actually going to turn in time.

Conclusion

And that's it really. If you follow all or some of the advice offered in *Foolproof Jumping Exercises*, you will undoubtedly be jumping better by the time you've worked your way through it. You can pick and choose which exercises apply more to you and your horse, or which will give you the most benefit to help you solve any little, or large, problems.

Remember that there are no quick fixes but once you have worked hard to establish a better mode of jumping, you shouldn't slide casually backwards into bad habits again.

Never underestimate the value of your helper's contribution to the success of the work, even if they just start off as a drudge, a pole putter-upper. Make sure they read *Foolproof Jumping Exercises* too; it will help them to understand what is required from horse and rider, they will learn more from every training and practice session and, if you are lucky, their interest and enthusiasm will enable you and your horse to achieve far more than you originally thought possible.

If you find your results starting to slip, dip into *Foolproof Jumping Exercises* once more; you are bound to find exactly the right work and advice to set you on track again.

And, most importantly, don't forget to enjoy it!

Index